MY MOTHER, MY DAUGHTER

MY MOTHER MY DAUGHTER

WOMEN SPEAK ABOUT RELATING ACROSS THE GENERATIONS

ELAINE K. McEWAN

Harold Shaw Publishers
Wheaton, Illinois

ISBN 0-87788-570-2

Library of Congress Cataloging-in-Publication Data

McEwan, Elaine K., 1941-
    My mother, my daughter : women speak out / Elaine K. McEwan.
      p.   cm.
    Includes bibliographical references.
    ISBN 0-87788-570-2
    1. Mothers and daughters—United States.   I. Title.
HQ755.85.M36 1992
306.874'3—dc20   91-42852
                                            CIP

99 98 97 96 95 94 93 92

10 9 8 7 6 5 4 3 2 1

To my daughter, Emily C. McEwan
To my mother, Viola A. Lantinga

Contents

Preface

M<small>Y SISTER WAS OUTSPOKEN WHEN SHE LEARNED I PLANNED TO</small>
write a book about mothers and daughters. "I find it interesting that
you would choose to write about that topic." There was more than a
touch of irony in her statement. I was estranged from our mother for
many years before she died. But that is precisely why I have written
this book.

I have many questions about the mother-daughter relationship.
Walking down a crowded city street, I catch a reflection of myself in
the store window. I don't see myself in that reflection but rather my
mother, looking as she did when she was my age, the parent of a
young adult daughter. I'm not displeased by the physical reflection.
My mother was an attractive, well-groomed woman, and I like the
way I look. The reflection gives me another dimension however—a
psychological and emotional one. If I look deep into the eyes of my
reflection, what do I really see? Am I my mother's daughter? She
was a housewife, content (or perhaps constrained) to live her life
defined almost solely by children and husband. My family has also
defined my life, but my careers (educator and author) bring a dimen-

sion and richness to my life that Mother rarely if ever enjoyed. Her self-worth and esteem seemed to come only from the accomplishments of her children. After my father died she discovered the artistic talents we always suspected she had and began painting. But after a brief flurry of success, she put her oils away and concentrated on a second husband. He was disapproving of the sights and smells of an artist's studio, and I was resentful of the haste with which she set aside her talents for a man. But why didn't we or couldn't we mend our relationship and come together again as mother and daughter?

My relationship with my own daughter, a young adult, is much different from the one I experienced with my mother. Emily and I are more open; we are more direct; we share both pain and joy on a deeper level than did my mother and I. But in a secret place in my mind and heart, I am worried. Will it last? Am I destined to repeat the mistakes of my relationship with my mother with my own daughter as she launches into adulthood?

Are we our mothers' daughters? What is the role of a mother in shaping her daughter's personality and identity as a woman? What can we do to build positive mother-daughter relationships with our own daughters and avoid the mistakes of our own pasts? Can we mend broken mother-daughter relationships? What can we learn from the experiences of others?

I was curious to know how other women like me felt about these important questions so I began to talk to friends about their mother-daughter relationships. A common thread ran through these conversations—women were eager to talk! Some had unhappy experiences to share; there were many tears shed over abusive mothers and rebellious daughters. Others waxed eloquent about the joys of their mother-daughter relationships; these women were convinced they had the answers to success.

❦

I decided to draw on a wider sample of women and ask them to put their observations in writing. Based on my research of the literature on mothers and daughters, I developed a questionnaire (see Appendix A). The questionnaire was designed for women who are both daughters and mothers—those of us in the middle.

Out of the one hundred twelve questionnaires that were sent out, eighty-eight were returned. Many women returned them with personal notes attached—they had spent hours reflecting on the dynamics of their own mother-daughter relationships. Others called to ask for extensions on my deadline. They needed time to call their mothers or talk to their daughters. Some found the experience exhilarating; others found it difficult and depressing. But those who completed it did so from their hearts, with honesty and clarity. I've learned from these women, and I hope you will also.

Introduction

I HAVE A WIDE CIRCLE OF WOMEN FRIENDS, AND HOW WE LOVE TO talk. The topics range from diets to death. But invariably we come back to the subject of our mothers and daughters. We can't decide whether we hate them or love them. But it's clear that our relationships with them make up the fabric of our daily lives. One minute we're ecstatic over a breakthrough in understanding, and the next minute we're in tears over what they're doing to us now. We're caught in the middle. While we desperately attempt to make sense of our own lives—our faith, marriages, and careers—we're pulled like rubberbands between mothers who don't always seem as grown-up as they should be and daughters who want to grow up overnight.

This intergenerational struggle has been examined by dozens of therapists and psychologists. They approach their studies from the Freudian, Jungian, and feminist perspectives—not always the most helpful perspectives for today's Christian woman. And sometimes only the bad relationships get noticed. Mothers and daughters who enjoy "storybook" relationships are often overlooked for the more bizarre pairs. In my own quest for the "truth" about the relationship between mothers and daughters I began by reading what others had written. But I also wanted to do some field research around the kitchen tables of my friends. The bibliography of items I examined and read to write this book contains over one hundred entries. I personally carried each volume home from the public library and paid tens of dollars in overdue book fines. The research and literature in the field of mothers and daughters is well represented in the chapters ahead. But so are the experiences of everyday women like you and me. Unfortunately, I didn't have the time to sit around eighty-eight kitchen tables and chat personally with everyone about their mothers and daughters. So I'm especially grateful to those women who consented to complete a lengthy questionnaire about their own personal mother-daughter relationships. (See Appendix A.) Some of the women are close personal friends, but dozens are strangers. Many are Christian authors, illustrators, leaders, and speakers. Some women volunteered to participate after hearing of the study from others. Some were college classmates I had not seen in years. Others were women I worked with on a daily basis.

In the chapters ahead we will explore the mother-daughter relationship from several perspectives. We'll look at what it means to be a woman and mother in our society; how mothers impact their daughters' development; the unique characteristics of mother-daughter relationships in childhood, adolescence, young adulthood, and adulthood; and suggestions for mending broken mother-daughter relationships.

The women who participated in this study have much to tell us about the state of mother-daughter relationships. They are the women in the middle. They are working through their own relationships with mothers while parenting as many as five daughters themselves. We'll hear in their own words about the unique joys and sorrows of being both a daughter and a mother. Let me introduce you to this fascinating group of women. Since reading each of their questionnaires, I feel as if I know them personally. While the crucial elements of their stories remain intact, all of their names and some descriptions have been changed to protect their privacy. (See Appendix B for more complete data.)

Their Ages

The youngest participant in the study was 32 and the oldest was 76. The majority of the respondents fell in the 36-55 age range (66%). Their mothers ranged in age from 49-99. Twenty-one of the respondents' mothers were deceased. Two lost their mothers in infancy, two in childhood, eight in young adulthood, and only two in middle age. The mothers of our respondents are a hardy and active group of women. Many have continued to work past retirement age.

Marital Status

Seventy-two (82%) of the participants were married. While the questionnaire did not specifically ask for information about spouses, over a third of the respondents volunteered positive comments about their marriage relationships. Four respondents were equally frank about their desperately unhappy marriages.

Education

The respondents were a well-educated group of women. All had received high-school diplomas. Almost 80% have at least a bachelor's degree. There were six nurses (R.N.), one lawyer (J.D.), and three doctors of education (Ed.D). Many had either obtained or were working on advanced degrees in midlife.

Religious Status

Fifty-one percent of the respondents (forty-five) professed either a personal commitment to Jesus Christ or a high degree of involvement in an evangelical church. Twenty-five percent were involved in mainline Protestant denominations and made no profession of personal faith. Ten percent of the participants were Catholic, 3% were Jewish, and 11% either attended no church or professed no religious faith.

Employment Status

Only four women (5%) had never worked after graduation from either high school or college. Over half (fifty-four of the women) were presently working, having continued to work throughout their child-rearing years or having resumed employment after children were older. Eleven women were working either part-time or at home in deference to personal preference or child-care needs. Eighteen women (20%) who had worked prior to marriage or family now were not working. The majority of those working were engaged in professional careers related to their educational preparation (nursing, law, social work, business management, education, art and design, library science, writing, consulting, counseling).

Daughters

The eighty-eight participants had a total of 169 daughters. While the majority of participants had only one or two daughters (74%), twenty-three women had three or more daughters, with two participants having five. Forty-two of the daughters are between the ages of birth and twelve. Another forty-two are adolescents (ages 12-18).

❧

Daughters older than the age of 18 were subdivided according to their marital/family status. Thirty-six were single; ten were married with no children; and twenty-nine had children. Ten (6%) of the daughters had divorced and were either single or remarried.

Status of Relationship with Mother

Thirty of the women (38%) characterized their relationships with their own mothers as generally excellent. These respondents sometimes had a brief period during adolescence or young adulthood when minor conflicts arose with their mothers, but the problems were generally resolved rather quickly, with no lasting effects.

Thirty-nine women (49%) rated relationships with their mothers as average. These respondents either had longer periods of discord with their mothers characterized by lasting problems or selected the category of good as opposed to excellent in the rating scale. The women who fell into this category appeared to be somewhat ambivalent about their relationships with their mothers. They weren't effusive in their praise of the relationship, but neither did they cite specific examples of conflict.

Ten women (13%) cited poor relationships with their mothers. Sometimes the problems began in early childhood or adolescence and grew worse, but in many cases problems that had remained dormant exploded once the subjects began to gain more independence and establish lives of their own. Some respondents whose mothers were deceased did not complete the status of relationship portions of the questionnaire, while others whose mothers had died in recent memory did so. This accounts for the difference in number of total respondents (eighty-eight) and the number of women who answered this question (seventy-nine). Typical minor problems causing conflict between the respondents and their mothers during adolescence included choices of clothing and friends, failure to take responsibility for personal possessions and living space, inappropriate eating habits, and breaking household rules. In young adulthood and adulthood, problems focused on larger lifestyle issues such as choice of a mate, choice of a church or spiritual value, or divorce. Many mother-daughter conflicts experienced by the participants were centered around key emotional and psychological issues: inability to give unconditional love, lack of physical demonstrations of love, dishonesty, no appreciation for accomplishments, and the need of mother for total control.

A third set of issues revolved around a dysfunctional mother who might be deeply depressed, alcoholic, anorexic, hostile and angry, or totally dependent.

Status of Relationships with Daughters

Most mother-daughter relationships seem to start out well. The women in this study have forty-two daughters between birth and twelve years of age, and 95% enjoy outstanding relationships with them. Only two women indicated a less-than-idyllic relationship with a young daughter. Adolescence, however, brings with it a sharp decline in the quality of the mother-daughter relationship. Of the forty-two adolescent daughters, only ten respondents (24%) indicated an excellent relationship with them, while thirty respondents (70%) ranked their relationship as good. Two (5%) ranked their relationship as poor.

The turning point for many mothers and daughters is adolescence. Only eight of the eighty-eight respondents (9%) indicated no decline in the quality of the relationship with their mother during adolescence and their present relationships with their own daughters are similar. Of the eighty-five daughters in the study who had passed through adolescence, only ten (12%) managed to do so without some type of conflict, albeit a minor one in most cases.

The arrival of a new generation does not seem to have changed the issues that cause mothers and adolescent daughters to part ways. The participants cited the following issues as common sources of conflict between them and their daughters: clothing, choice of friends, cleaning room, following house rules, moodiness, lack of goals or focus in life, lack of responsibility, and weight control.

The onset of young adulthood brings a slight increase in the number of mothers who rank their relationship as excellent (38%). Fifty-two percent of the mothers rank their relationship with young adult daughters as good. Five women (10%) rated their relationship as poor.

As daughters become adults in their own right, mothers perceive the relationships they have with them in an even more positive light. Mothers rated their relationships as excellent with eighteen of the thirty-seven adult daughters, good with sixteen, and poor with only three. The perceptions of the subjects' relationships with their own daughters is far more positive than their perceived experiences with their own mothers, however. Respondents believe that they personally are doing a better job of mothering their daughters than their own mothers did for them.

The women cited the following issues as sources of conflict between them and their young adult/adult daughters: choice of mate, alternate lifestyle (lesbian/living with someone), eating disorders, drugs/alcohol, abortion. This list reflects many new concerns for mothers in the 90s. Mothers also cited conflicts caused when family structures changed due to death, divorce, and remarriage. Young adult daughters seem particularly vulnerable to any shifts in family stability.

While in most cases a conflict between the respondent and her mother did not necessarily correspond to a similar conflict between

❦

respondent and daughter, a pattern emerged in thirteen (15%) of the questionnaires in which respondents had conflicts or pointed out faults of a similar nature in both their mothers and daughters.

Status as Caretakers

Twenty-two of the eighty-eight respondents (25%) either have in the past or are presently in caretaking relationships with their mothers. In some cases, their mothers live in their homes, in some cases respondents send financial support, and in others they visit regularly in nursing homes or hospitals. Still other respondents feel the psychological responsibility of giving emotional support to a failing mother.

On Use of Counselor/Therapist to Assist in Solving Problems

Six of the eighty-eight respondents (7%) have sought help from a counselor or therapist. The problems they have sought to resolve include alcoholism, suicide, anorexia, divorce, and dysfunctional family and marital relationships.

Mothers and Daughters: Women Speak Out

You have been briefly introduced to the eighty-eight women who participated in this study. In the chapters ahead you'll hear more about them as we compare their experiences to descriptions and studies of other mother-daughter relationships. We'll begin by looking at what it means to be a Christian woman and mother in today's society. Changing views on the role of women in the church, the workplace, and even the home are having a major impact on the

❦

mother-daughter relationship. Our respondents are caught in the middle once again. Their mothers espoused the traditional views of marriage and family. But they are discovering for themselves the challenges and personal rewards in serving God in leadership roles their mothers never dreamed of. Meanwhile their daughters are struggling with economic and societal pressures to "do and have it all." Chapter Two will examine motherhood and the role women play in impacting their daughters' development. What are the psychological dynamics that take place when mothers interact with their daughters? Are women born to motherhood or do they have to learn along the way? Those are some questions we'll explore together.

Chapters Three through Six will describe the unique characteristics of the mother-daughter relationship in four different developmental periods: childhood, adolescence, young adulthood, and adulthood. We'll get to know more about the eighty-eight participants and their mothers and daughters as we hear them talk about sex, food, fathers, faith, and the future.

You will discover as you read that there are many mothers and daughters caught in vicious cycles of mother-blame and dysfunctional behavior patterns. Perhaps you'll recognize yourself in some of the case studies. In Chapters Seven and Eight, we'll look at ways to break destructive cycles and mend the broken mother-daughter relationship.

My Mother, My Daughter: Women Speak Out does not beg to be read from cover to cover. If you're the mother of an adolescent, skip right to Chapter Four. Given the problems most mothers and daughters face during this period, you need help, and you need it fast. After you've discovered that you're in good company and there is hope for the future, go back to the beginning and read in a more leisurely fashion. If you're caught in the middle of a heart-breaking

❧

relationship with either your mother or daughter, then read Chapters Seven and Eight at once. Begin thinking and praying about how you can come to grips with the challenges you face. I hope your own mother-daughter relationships will be enriched as a result of reading this book. Mine were as a result of writing it!

Chapter One

Being a Woman
What Does it Mean?

The Greeks believed beauty was to be found in harmony,
in dignity, and women who accept themselves
in all the stages of life achieve that balance.
ANNE ROIPHE, "The Beauty Trap," in *Family Circle*

I FIRST HAD THE IDEA FOR THIS BOOK IN 1988. I WAS ATTENDING
the twenty-fifth reunion of my graduating class from Wheaton College. I was delighted to see my fellow "brave daughters true," as we
were called in our Alma Mater song. We had graduated from college
in 1963, and most of us were born the year that World War II began.
Our mothers came of age during the war years. We would face the
turbulent 60s while we attempted to find ourselves. Identity for most
of us in 1963 meant finding a man and getting married, and dozens
of us managed to achieve that goal at almost the same time as we
received our diplomas. In spite of our traditional upbringings we

would find ourselves on the cutting edge of the many changes that would occur in the 60s and 70s.

Gathered around the buffet table during our first evening together, we eagerly shared stories of midlife advanced degrees and transitions from dependent to independent. I had recently received my doctorate in educational administration. Another had just completed medical school and was doing a residency in obstetrics and gynecology. Still another was serving her fifth term on the city council. Many of us had worked prior to childbearing but had taken time from our work lives to be full-time mothers. We were discovering our gifts and talents anew and taking them into the world of work. Our mothers were aging while our daughters were just beginning college, facing a world that was much different, particularly in its attitudes and expectations toward young women.

A recent study by the U.S. Bureau of the Census titled "Work and Family Patterns of American Women" is based upon life patterns of 40.6 million women born between 1920 and 1954 who have been married at least once and have children. The report indicates that I and others like me in the class of 1963 were the first generation to step out of traditional roles for American women. Many of us grew up during the war years with Rosie the Riveter and saw our mothers going off to help in the war effort. Even though most of them returned to the kitchen after the war, the seeds had been sown. We came of age during the 1960s when the birth control pill was available and a sexual revolution swept the country.

❧ In recent years, women have experienced more freedom . . . freedom to develop gifts, pursue dreams, and become leaders in areas that used to be off-limits.—**R. Ruth Barton,** *Women Like Us*

❦

Our role as Christian women was even more puzzling. The church often had us relegated to teaching Sunday school and making casseroles. How did our newly discovered independence mesh with this mindset?

I began to speculate about mother-daughter relationships in the context of all of this change. We were just beginning to find ourselves, and now we had to face launching adolescent daughters who didn't listen to us while at the same time relating to and caring for aging mothers who didn't understand us. Mother-daughter relationships were a major source of both the joy and the sorrow in our lives.

While other writing projects and family commitments forced me to table the idea, the prospect of looking at women like myself and examining the relationships they have with their mothers and daughters continued to tantalize me. And so in this chapter, we'll take the first step in understanding the complex relationships we have with our mothers and daughters—understanding what it means to be a woman in today's world. For only if we understand and appreciate ourselves can we be the best of mothers and daughters.

What Does It Mean to Be a Woman in Today's World?

It's not easy being a woman. There are still many men (and women) who are secretly delighted when a boy is born into their family. Ann Oakley discovered while interviewing new mothers in London in the mid-1970s that a staggering 44% of mothers would admit to being disappointed in the birth of a daughter. Only 8% were disappointed with a son.[1] The belief that males are more important and valuable than females pervades many societies, including the United States. And once we survive our rude welcome into the world, our sex-role stereotyping begins at birth. Thirty parents were interviewed twenty-four hours after the birth of their first baby. Although the babies themselves, when diapered, clearly had no obvious male or female traits, the parents of girls rated their babies as softer and smaller and described them as prettier and cuter and more beautiful than did the parents of boy babies.[2]

Parents have different aspirations for their sons and daughters. According to one study, twice as many parents want their sons, rather than their daughters, to be ambitious and hardworking. Fathers are more likely to want their sons to be career-oriented than their daughters, and they are more disapproving of a son who fails to acquire high-achievement goals.[3]

In addition to the stereotypes and expectations laid upon us by the secular world, we must also contend with another set of expectations—those that come from the Christian media. Marabel Morgan tells us we must be the "total woman"—ever ready to meet the sexual needs of our spouses as they enter the front door. Other Christian leaders and authors want to keep us at home, barefoot, and pregnant. And Mary Pride would like us to be simultaneously schooling our children and running our own business at home. Even God's Word seems to send us mixed messages, telling us on the one hand to keep our mouths shut and on the other hand to sharpen our business skills in the marketplace with energy and hard work.

What Does It Mean to Be a Woman in Today's Church?

My friend Jill recently shared her thoughts with me about this issue.

> I grew up in a home where my dad treated my mother as an equal. My father gave strong spiritual leadership to our family, but he was also happy to change diapers and wash dishes. Though I grew up in a very

conservative, evangelical setting, I saw women using their gifts quite freely. My mother was actively involved in church leadership as a deacon and as church treasurer. My grandfather, a conservative fundamentalist pastor, often had women evangelists and preachers in his pulpit. I never recall this being an issue or a problem. God greatly blessed the ministries of my pastor grandfather and my missionary father.

Then God gave me a great marriage to a husband who has continually affirmed me, first as a wife and mother and then, as our children grew older, encouraging me to stretch my horizons educationally and professionally. Though I have a very satisfying part-time job now, my roles as wife and mother continue to be my greatest joy.

Jill has faced the issue of the role of women in the church directly as her congregation has struggled to define a leadership role for women in their church. She recently presented her views to the congregation in a public meeting:

I appreciate the high view of Scripture which is part of our church tradition. I want to be obedient to Scripture. I admit that I am puzzled by passages such as 1 Corinthians 14 and 1 Timothy 2, which seem to place strict constraints on women. If these passages are affirmed as normative for our practice today, we as women must radically change our role in the church. We must be silent in the church. This means we should not teach Sunday school or sing special music or give testimonies. We must learn in silence as women did in the Jewish synagogues. We must also cover our heads and refrain from wearing gold or pearls or expensive clothing. While I don't like these restrictions, I think I would be willing to submit to them if I really believed these passages to be normative for today. Certainly it would mean far less work for us as women and a lot more work for the men in our congregation!

❧

But I also see a whole body of Scripture that affirms women as co-heirs of the grace of God. I see examples such as Miriam, Deborah, Huldah, the daughters of Philip, Priscilla, and Phoebe. These women proclaimed the Word of God, taught, led, and served. I also see the example of Jesus—God's central message to humanity. Jesus turned the hierarchical system of his day on its head, showing amazingly respectful treatment of women. The central message of Paul's writings is freedom in Christ, summed up in Galatians 3:28: "There is neither Jew nor Greek, slave nor free, male nor female, for you are all one in Christ Jesus." As I allow Scripture to interpret Scripture, I conclude that the restrictions Paul placed on women were culturally bound to a specific situation. I pray that together we can affirm each other's gifts, spurring one another on to fan into flame the gifts God has given to each one.

What Roles Have the Women's Liberation Movement and Feminism Played in Our Lives?

All eighty-eight women who completed the questionnaire answered the question: "How would you characterize your views toward 'women's liberation'?" with nearly unanimous support of the gains the women's movement has made in the areas of equal employment opportunity and equal pay for equal work. A sixty-one-year-old artist and mother of seven (two daughters) who has only recently seen the last of her children leave the nest said it best:

I support the idea of equal compensation for women. My mother worked for thirty-five years and never received the salary that a man would have received.

❧

But she, like many others, is concerned that the women's movement is chipping away at the family structure, taking women out of the home and putting children into day care. While her daughters were younger, Diane was a stay-at-home mom. Now she works full-time as a school secretary and wants equal rights for moms who stay at home:

> The only choice feminists seem to reject is that of being a wife and mother. I strongly believe we are seeing the results of the absent mother in today's youth.

Age does not seem to be the determining factor in views either positive or negative about the women's movement. Younger mothers in the 25-35 age range were just as conservative as the older respondents. A registered nurse before her three daughters were born, Tami, 34, believes women's liberation has been negative.

> It has made many full-time homemakers feel inadequate and unfulfilled. It has made women put themselves before their husbands and children, which is contrary to God's plan.

A high-school English teacher who began working full-time when her children went off to school, Jayne, 47, applauds the attention drawn to increased opportunities for women to make choices:

> Women ought to be able to decide what's best for them, whether it be a career as a mother/homemaker or in combination with a career outside the home.

There are a number of women in the study who could be characterized as feminists. They lobby for change in their churches, belong
to Christian feminist groups, and enjoy egalitarian relationships in
their marriages. They are not angry militants. In fact, they decry the
overly assertive and aggressive approaches taken by some feminist
groups, yet they clearly represent an active voice in lobbying for
change in the home and the church as well as the workplace. "I
consider myself 'liberated' and am a strong proponent of women's
issues," says Marge, a school social worker.

Some women are grateful for what the women's movement has
done for them. A fifty-year-old school administrator and mother of
one young adult daughter had this to say: "I enjoy the privileges of
women's lib, a satisfying career, and opportunities to travel. I've
even begun to feel more tolerant about chauvinism." A woman entre-
preneur who is beginning to enjoy the first blush of success in her
new business says, "I'm happy it's here and happy it's still coming."
She has become a self-proclaimed biblical feminist and rues the day
she deferred to male leadership when asked to teach a Sunday school
class some twenty years ago.

Some women regret their own personal lack of opportunity to
experience the benefits of the movement: "I'm sad that I haven't
been socialized to express myself." Others clearly have no difficulty
telling it like they think it is: "My role is not to cater to please the
men in my life," said a forty-two-year-old who has recently traded in
her volunteer badges for a full-time job as a publicist.

The subject of women's liberation is a controversial one for many
women. Those I surveyed have not yet fully integrated their biblical
beliefs, societal expectations, marriage relationships, and the prac-
ticalities of life (75% of the respondents are currently employed—
62% of them full-time). But they "bristle" (a word used by several of

them) at the stance of reactionary feminist groups. They reject the anger and militancy that have characterized some aspects of the feminist movement, and they clearly reject the views of the New Right, which ignores the women who must work out of financial necessity and through no choice of their own. They are slightly uneasy about sounding unchristian in their views and nearly always include a disclaimer in their responses:

I'm in favor of equal opportunities and salaries for women, *but* I'm against women leaving children to go to war.

I don't like the anger and militancy that characterize the feminists, *but* I do believe the church has misinterpreted the Scriptures in this area and there should be equal opportunity for women.

I believe a woman should have the right to do any job outside the home; *however*, I do not believe she should try to rule over her husband.

I'm for equal pay for equal work, *but* I don't think you can have it all.

I have mixed emotions. I want it both ways.

I appreciate equal pay and opportunity, *but* I hate abortion and extremes.

When asked how their own personal views differed from those of their daughters and mothers, the respondents were in the middle of the continuum. They see their daughters trying to do it all, and their responses range from amazement and pride to disapproval.

My daughters both try to juggle homemaking, mothering, and some outside-the-home work. They seem to feel they must contribute to the family income. I *will* say that their husbands are more involved with household tasks and child care.

I'm pleased that young fathers seem to be getting in the child-care "act" more these days.

They see their mothers as more traditional, even Victorian, with regard to their views on the role of women in the world. They are beginning to question those views while attempting to construct their own sense of reality.

I don't know if my mother had any views. She certainly never verbalized them. She was "sick" a lot of times, and now I wonder if that might have been her way of protesting her oppression.

Meanwhile, their daughters are leaving them far behind.

At the age of twelve my daughter gets upset if the word "mankind" is used in the worship service and still bears a grudge against her school principal for asking for some "strong boys" to help with a physical task.

Women are in the middle of change, and that change is nowhere more reflected than in the dozens of transitions through which our lives are going on a daily basis.

What Transitions or Phases Characterize the Lives of Most Women?

Rosemary is an amazing woman. At the age of 69, she has reared four daughters, now ages 42, 40, 37, and 36. They have each attended college, and two have degrees in nursing. They're all happily married with families of their own. No small achievement. There are few mothers who can make such claims. An elementary school teacher for over thirty years, Rosemary left home at 14 to live with relatives so she could attend school. She is a strong and steady woman. She has needed strength to rear her daughters alone. Her abusive and mentally ill husband left home when the girls were in elementary school. Rosemary kept the house together and supported them. She and her husband didn't divorce until ten years later, but Rosemary still remembers his authoritarian approach to childrearing. She survived a bout with cancer and planned her retirement with care. She traveled with friends—Alaska, Sweden, Europe. She's never been one to avoid a challenge. Her mother died last October at the age of 99—another transition for Rosemary. Shortly thereafter she entered yet another stage in her life—dating, after being single for twenty-eight years. She shyly introduces her husband-to-be to friends and relatives. Her love and excitement are obvious. She will become a bride in the spring.

There are several predictable transitions in a woman's life— entering first grade at the age of 6, graduating from high school at the age of 18, preparing for a career following graduation or attending college, marrying during the twenties or thirties, having a first child sometime thereafter, and retiring from work or career at age 62 or 65. Rosemary moved through each of these transitions. But they do not begin to define the life that has been *hers*.

❦

In addition to the age-graded events that circumscribe a woman's life, there are historic events that influence societal norms and subsequently impact a woman's life: the Great Depression, World War II, Vietnam, Women's Liberation, the Cold War. All of these events or movements influence public opinion and become part of the fabric of our lives. Rosemary has seen a whirlwind of change in her 69 years. Her adolescence took place during the Great Depression; she came of age during World War II; she reared her children during the turbulent 60s; and she's come to grips with the women's movement as she's fended for herself both at work and in the community. Surviving the social changes has given her a bedrock of personal values. Her strong faith undergirds it all.

A third category of events cannot be predicted. Rosemary has had a number of such events in her life as well—divorce, death, and illness. These events offer the potential for growth and development on the part of the individual, and Rosemary rose to each occasion, growing and changing as a woman.

The transitions in our lives can be either internally or externally motivated. In Rosemary's case her remarriage was internally motivated. This act of commitment after years of living alone was an exciting adventure, one she faced with happy anticipation. The adjustments, I'm sure, will be many as she is in the process of becoming yet another Rosemary. Sometimes our transitions are externally motivated. I presently am living through one such transition. My husband of twenty-six years died last December of pancreatic cancer. I had anticipated the empty-nest transition as our last child entered college in the fall, but nothing could have prepared me for the shock of widowhood that was thrust upon me with only three months' warning. Now I face an empty house in addition to an empty nest.

❦

The Five Stages of a Woman's Life

Mercer, Nichols, and Doyle have written of these transitions in a fascinating volume, *Transitions in a Woman's Life: Major Life Events in Developmental Context.* They interviewed eighty women over the age of 60 and asked them to recall all they could about their life histories. Based on this information they hypothesized five major developmental periods in the lives of women, periods when major life-shaping events are occurring:

1. **16-25:** Launching into Adulthood/Breaking Away
2. **26-30:** Leveling/Young versus Old
3. **36-40:** Liberating/Attachment versus Separateness
4. **61-65:** Regeneration/Redirection
5. **76-80:** Creativity versus Destructiveness[4]

The Launching into Adulthood Period is characterized by graduations, marriages, entrance into careers, and becoming mothers for the first time. During the Leveling Period, women turn to building their own families, working through marriage problems, and becoming involved in community activities. During the Liberating Period, women return to school, return to work, and feel less tied down by the demands of childrearing.

The next major transitional period, Regeneration/Redirection, occurs when either the woman or husband retires from work. Deaths of family members and friends become more frequent, and many women begin new careers. The period from ages 76-80, Creativity versus Destructiveness, offers women the opportunity to achieve a sense of integrity about their lives. Women in this period have the

❦

opportunity to resolve creatively any conflicts about the worth of their lives and to prepare for death.[5]

Transitions for women include the deaths of children, husbands, and parents; births of handicapped children; life-threatening illnesses; advanced degrees and career satisfaction; divorce and abuse; spiritual renewal; and psychological rebirth. Julie, a children's librarian and mother of a young adult daughter, put it this way: "It doesn't depend on what happens to us, but how we handle each stage."

Let's examine the five stages. Where have the women of today been and where are they going?

The Launching into Adulthood Period

The period of Launching into Adulthood is definitely a challenge for all women. Going off to college was the first transition for Kristina, who now gives private piano lessons and has just packed away her mother-of-the-bride dress in her now-empty home.

> In going to college from a small town, I was introduced to a wider, wiser, and more sophisticated world.

Margaret, an artist and mother of a two-year-old, wasn't quite ready for her launching.

> I think I grew up too fast and became a wife and mother too soon. The step into motherhood was unexpected. Sometimes I really miss being the irresponsible, creative individual who only has to watch out for herself.

Melissa, too, was skyrocketed into change. She lost both her husband and her first daughter in her early twenties while pregnant with her second daughter. She has turned that tragedy into a speaking ministry to others dealing with grief.

Some really don't make the transition until later. "I finished adolescence at about age 32," laughs Tonya, a social worker who is also trying to help her daughter make the break from home to college. Carolyn, a former teacher of the gifted, faced an especially difficult transition during her adolescent years. Her father died, and her mother became depressed and ill. At the age of 40 she is still mourning those losses, unable to leave them behind.

The Leveling Period

Many young mothers are in the second stage of transition—in the Leveling Period. Beth, a former elementary teacher, now stays at home with her two daughters. She is active in community organizations that minister to young mothers, and she is making a new career in parenting.

> I think I went through a significant change when I had my first child. I became more responsible and much more concerned about my actions and the things I said. I realized that my children watched and learned from everything I did and said. Therefore I needed to always try to set a good example for them.

Sandy, a speech pathologist, matured psychologically during her thirties.

> I realized that only I was capable of making things happen in my life, that I had to make my own personal decisions and that I had a right to meet my own needs as well as those of others.

❧

The Liberation Period

Middle age is a time of leveling out and coming to grips with who we really are as women. For those of us in happy marriages with grown daughters, there is now time to reflect on our accomplishments and feel good about ourselves.

I'm comfortable and secure with who I am—forgiving of my faults and those of others.

I'm more confident and independent now.

I'm more patient and tolerant, less critical.

But for those women who have faced serious illness, divorce, or tragedy, the changes are much deeper.

A serious illness three years ago changed my life forever. Before I got sick I was somewhat of a Sunday Christian. My illness made me put my priorities in their right order. I asked Jesus into my heart and have never been able to satisfy my hunger for the Word, since being born-again is the best thing that can happen to anyone.

Becoming a diabetic fourteen years ago has forced me to lead a very disciplined life.

I no longer allow myself to become depressed or suicidal because of rejection. Now I work through the rejection and build myself up instead of tearing myself apart.

❧

My cancer surgery really made an impact on me. I've learned to enjoy and appreciate each day—my family and what they mean to me.

Divorce has softened me. I've become less judgmental and more compassionate.

The Regeneration/Redirection Period

Women over sixty years of age are facing transitions of yet another kind.

I'm now going through the adjustment of having my husband home since he retired. I'm working at being more flexible with my daily schedule and being available to do things and go places together.

A mother of seven whose last child just left the nest is enjoying her own interests for the first time in her life: "I'm doing a lot of art work—practically a career."

The Creativity versus Destructiveness Period

Women in their mid-seventies or older often finally have the opportunity to slow down and reflect on the value of their lives—the things they have done, the persons whose lives they have touched. Some live in sorrow and regret; others are continually challenged, like this woman:

I have learned and keep learning and hope I never stop learning. I think being rigid and locking my ideas in cement can kill relationships.

How Can I Do It All?

Women's liberation has come with a price. We're now expected to do it all: have a career, raise children, survive the rat race, and still be nurturing and supportive. When I was growing up my own mother socialized me in some very specific ways. I was trained to be psychologically "there" twenty-four hours a day for my spouse and children. I was socialized to keep my negative feelings to myself. I was socialized to believe that all of the family's household needs were my responsibility. I was socialized around the expectation that I would someday be a wife and mother.

Fortunately for my survival in my career, my father, whom I followed around from the age of twelve, also socialized me. I had the best of both worlds. He socialized me to be strong. He socialized me to figure out what I wanted and to go after it. He socialized me to be competitive and learn how to say "no." As you can imagine, from time to time I suffer some role conflict; which hat should I be wearing today? I've got to do it all, and I've got to do it right. When my husband was alive we would frequently discuss topics related to role conflicts and priorities. The central issue always remained the same—slow down, say no, and remember what's most important in life. He was always the voice of reason and could cut through to basic issues. In addition, he pitched in, cooked meals, changed diapers, and was understanding when there were no dinners, clean clothes, or dust-free surfaces.

Many women aren't as blessed as I was. Faced with the challenge, they rise to it. And consequently they strive to be Superwomen. I've been there on occasion myself. It can't be done. As women we need to learn the lesson of being good to ourselves.

I learned to be good to myself when my two children were very small. I learned to take long hot baths with a good book. They were

❦

my mini-vacations where I could be rejuvenated and refreshed. The door was locked, and I couldn't be disturbed. Oh, they could knock, but I told them to go ask their dad. I found friends with whom to trade babysitting, and I treated myself to a solitary luncheon or a quiet read in the library. I've continued that practice even though I'm all alone in the house now. My husband is dead, and my children are away at college. Now my treats are weekly massages and manicures. I don't really *need* either of these indulgences, but, if only for a brief moment, someone else is ministering to my body and refreshing my spirit. I'm being good to myself.

What If I Don't Feel Good about Myself?

The majority of the eighty-eight women who completed the questionnaire have positive self-images, feel capable, competent, and proud of what they've attained. They are able to meet the challenges that life brings. They demonstrate that ability through rearing daughters, reaching career goals, developing relationships with their spouses and family members, and rising above untold tragedies. But there were some individuals who ached to be validated, cried out for success, and yearned for some feeling of self-worth. What can be said to these and other women (perhaps even you) whose lives are troubled and unfulfilled? Some of them have been reared from childhood with the belief that they will only be worth loving if they put the needs of everyone else before their own. They see value in themselves primarily as it is reflected in the eyes of others. They have no ego. Since my husband died, I've done a lot of thinking about the female ego. I didn't have a particularly well-developed one when we married. Perhaps none of us do at the age of 23. I believed I should say "yes" to everyone and what I felt or believed about an issue was less important than what any other individual believed. But

the Lord blessed me with a husband who nurtured my ego development, encouraged my self-esteem, and believed that I could do anything I set my mind to. He spent twenty-three years preparing me for
the time I would walk up the stairs alone at night. He encouraged me
to get a doctorate when I thought in terms of lesser goals. He pushed
me to take the risk of writing books. And he was always there to pick
me up when I fell. I only hope that he would have said the same
thing about me as a wife.

By one definition "ego" is self-centeredness and egotism. But in
the psychological sense "ego" is that important sense of self and
self-worth that is critical to healthy development and participation in
relationships with others. In her book, *The Female Ego: The Hidden
Power Women Possess but Are Afraid to Use,* Susan Price points out
that a healthy ego is the foundation of high self-esteem. She believes,
and I concur, that having a healthy ego gives you problem-solving
abilities, energy, confidence, and a clear sense of identity.[6] Next to
my strong faith, it's my ego that is most important in meeting the
challenges of widowhood. I face each day with two very powerful
messages in my brain: *God loves me,* and *I love myself.* Both messages are important. Because of my place in Christ, a woman made
in his image and loved by him, I have a solid sense of self-worth. I
hold a favored position—the daughter of the heavenly Father.
Having a healthy ego doesn't mean you're perfect; it means you like
yourself the way you are. Liking and affirming ourselves as women
is a critical prerequisite for good mothering—especially of
daughters.

❧ The people I know who truly like themselves as persons, apart
   from their roles in life as husband, wife, parent, or job-holder, are
   those who have learned to be honest with themselves and who

❦

to some degree understand themselves.—**Cecil G. Osborne,** ***The Art of Learning to Love Yourself***

Was I Born to Be a Mother?

Most of us were socialized for almost two decades to prepare for our role as mothers. So how come it's so hard? Why do we make so many mistakes? Why aren't we happy all the time? Why don't our daughters appreciate our great worth and wisdom? In the next chapter we'll examine just what motherhood is and, in the words of a popular book, "what it does to your mind." We'll begin to look at the unique aspects of mothering other females, the daughters that God has sent into our lives.

For more information . . .

Adeney, Miriam. *A Time for Risking: Priorities for Women.* Portland, Oreg.: Multnomah Press, 1987.

Gundry, Patricia. *Woman Be Free!* Grand Rapids, Mich.: Zondervan Publishing, 1977.

Martin, Faith. *Call Me Blessed: The Emerging Christian Woman.* Grand Rapids, Mich.: Wm. B. Eerdmans Publishing Co., 1988.

Reapsome, Martha. *A Woman's Path to Godliness.* Nashville: Oliver Nelson, 1986.

CHAPTER TWO

Motherhood
Myth and Reality

Judicious mothers will always keep in mind that they are the first book read, and the last put aside, in every child's library.
C. LENOX RAMOND

MOTHERS ARE OFTEN DEPICTED IN FAIRY TALES AND MOVIES IN blacks and whites. They are either good or bad. The good mother is selfless, kind, and nurturant. The "bad" mother, as seen in the image of Cinderella's wicked stepmother, is vain, selfish, sadistic, neglectful, and abusive. But most of us are somewhere in between. On the good days, when I was a new mother, I could have auditioned for a Kodak commercial. Music was playing softly in the background as I rocked near the sunlit window and read nursery rhymes aloud. On the bad days, I wanted to return to my former life where people appreciated my intelligence and hard work and where a job completed did not have to be redone all over again the next day.

My personal romantic dream of motherhood lasted for about two weeks after we brought our first child, Emily, home from the hospital. She was the ideal "good" baby for that two weeks. She slept almost all of the time. I can remember saying to myself in a smug, self-satisfied way, "This is a piece of cake. I wonder what all the fuss is about."

Then Emily showed us the other side of her personality—one we would grow to know better in the years to come. She turned her nights and days around. She cried nonstop into the wee hours of the morning. She refused to be comforted by anything her frantic parents tried. She nursed every two or three hours, leaving me feeling like a used-up cow. Our delightful pink bundle had turned into a screeching terror. As an author of books on parenting, I share a trait in common with many authors of that genre: we tend to focus on the positives and minimize the negatives. There were, however, *many* negatives in my early days as a mother. While I was reading aloud nonstop, as I recommend to parents in *How to Raise a Reader,* there were moments when I wondered if I'd ever get to read another adult book. In between playing the games I suggest in *Will My Child Be Ready for School?* I was sure that I would never be an interesting or attractive person again. My husband left each morning and commuted to the city. Sometimes I felt as though I'd been left behind on a desert island.

> ❧ Mothering does have its many pleasurable moments, but those come only with a total commitment of the will to weather all the sticky times in between.—**Stephen and Janet Bly,** *How to Be a Good Mom*

I don't mean to suggest that those feelings were pervasive. *Au contraire.* On many days motherhood made me feel fulfilled, radiant,

❦

grateful, and blessed. But a recurring dream that I had no difficulty analyzing found me curled up in my own mother's lap wanting to be comforted and nurtured myself. I was scared about the heavy burden of responsibility that faced me. If we speak the truth about motherhood (and many mothers never have that option or even exercise it), we must admit that on many occasions we feel devastated and lonely. We feel trapped, used-up, tired, fat, incompetent, vulnerable, and boring. Freud viewed women as being passive, narcissistic, dependent, nurturant, and happy only when they were being protected under the wing of a man. I don't agree with Freud for many reasons, especially because I never felt that way. At the times when we need them most, our husbands are often feeling a different set of pressures. They may withdraw from us and react with impatience and anger. Only now, with the perspective of twenty-one years and my own sense of responsibility for two children in college, can I empathize with my husband's vulnerability as a new father. I saw him as strong and all-knowing and couldn't understand his sudden mood shifts and fits of temperament. Now I know he was worried about taking over the full support of two dependent females and having to always be "the strong one."

Motherhood, particularly when it involves daughters, is a tricky business. In the pages ahead we'll explore the different facets of motherhood and discover how being the mother of a daughter can further define and enhance your own role as a woman.

How Does Society View Motherhood?

My mother didn't have much of a problem deciding whether or not she was going to be a mother. She got married and I was born a year later. My situation was different. My husband and I consciously postponed parenthood for five years. Then we carefully planned the

❧

birth of a second child two years later. The advent of birth control pills changed many of the options for the women of my generation.

When I got pregnant in 1970 I didn't have a decision to make about continuing to work; they hired another teacher to replace me. Today nearly every job or career has some maternity leave options as a given. My daughter will face yet another set of choices when she anticipates motherhood. Will she continue to work after her children are born? There was never any question in my mind that I would stay at home while my children were of preschool age. But once they entered first grade, I couldn't wait to get back to work.

The mother of the 1990s is significantly different from her counterpart in the 40s, 50s, and even the 60s. She is far less likely to be a homemaker living with her employed husband and their three or four children in the suburbs like I was from 1970-1978. That kind of woman represents fewer than 10% of today's American families. The typical contemporary mother is likely to be in the workforce. Sixty percent of American mothers work for pay. Fifty percent of that group have children under the age of three. The sample of women I interviewed are also working. Seventy-five percent are presently employed full-time, and most find their work to be a major source of satisfaction. Most of the women who are working part-time or not at all have preschool or school-age children or are of retirement age.

Today the typical American mother is quite likely to be divorced, separated, or never married and also poor. Those I surveyed are atypical in this regard. While 17% of the respondents have been divorced or widowed, 11% have remarried. The women who participated represent a privileged group who still enjoy the economic, psychological, and social benefits of being part of a couple.

The enormous debate and controversy that surrounded the Equal Rights Amendment and that continues to swirl around the effects of

❧

maternal employment are evidence that motherhood and our rights and responsibilities as mothers are critical domestic policy questions. Selma Fraiberg, author of *Every Child's Birthright: In Defense of Mothering*, advocates full-time mothering for three years. Burton White, Harvard psychologist and author of *The First Three Years*, would concur. Other more moderate parenting experts like T. Berry Brazleton qualify their advice with the need for "quality time" and cite research that states there is no evidence that this very early period in the relationship between mother and child is the sole determinant or even the major determinant of the developmental outcome of the early years. Each woman is faced with balancing the questions of economic necessity, personal needs for self-expression and, the most important of all factors, her child, in order to reach her personal decision.

Are We Born to Motherhood?

Depending on who you read or talk to, there are three ways to explain motherhood. We either do it because we can't help ourselves, because we've been socialized by our culture to do it, or because we try it, like it, and get good at it.

The biological view

The biological view of motherhood says that, as women, we're born to motherhood. We have that "biological time clock" ticking away in our bodies and will not be fulfilled until we have borne children. This view says that we're uniquely designed and innately skilled to nurture and raise children. It may even suggest in its more radical forms that no one else, not fathers, not day-care providers, not siblings, nor aunts, can "mother" the way one's real mother can "mother." As one who enjoyed mothering from aunts, uncles, and

❦

other extended family members, I have to question whether this theory offers the total picture with regard to motherhood.

The psychological view

A second theoretical perspective, the psychoanalytic view of motherhood, suggests that we learn to mother from our culture. If our culture expects us to teach our children to hunt and gather, we'll rise to the occasion. If our culture expects us to teach obedience, as did the slave culture in the South in order to protect children from the cruelty of slaveholders, we'll answer to those marching orders as well. Today, our culture is sending out thousands of messages, some of them quite mixed, about what to teach children. We don't even agree on what to teach in the school setting. At home, it's even more difficult. But as mothers we continue to try to please and do what the experts tell us we should. In the 50s we weren't supposed to pick up crying babies. They would be spoiled. We didn't. Today, we're encouraged to provide as much nurturing and bonding as possible. "Don't worry about spoiling your child," the experts tell us. In the 50s we weren't supposed to teach our children at home. "Leave that to us," the experts told us. Now we're encouraging parents to expose their children to as many early learning opportunities as possible.

The social learning view

The third perspective is drawn from the social learning school of thought. It posits that mothers and children must learn to relate to each other and that neither the mother nor child have instincts for caregiving or attachment. They must be learned together.

I'd have a hard time if someone asked me to choose only one theory or view from which to operate. Although I felt my biological

❦

clock ticking away at the age of thirty, I don't know if that was biology, culture, or the need to try something that was new and exciting. As a new mother, I certainly didn't rely on my instincts all of the time. I was a voracious reader and consulted every expert I could find. I'll confess to being influenced by many. I'd like to think I had a generous dose of common sense and no small guidance from the Lord as I did my mothering as well. But I do feel, like the social learning theorists, that motherhood has been a magnificent learning experience for both me and my children. The connections I feel with them do not come solely from our biological ties or our cultural similarities. They come from our shared experiences, our attempts to solve problems together, and the need to understand who we are and what we want to be as a family. You can make your own decision.

What Does Motherhood Do to Our Minds?

Motherhood definitely changed me as a person. I didn't pass through twenty-one years of parenting unscathed and untouched. I emerged as someone different. Just as the marriage relationship changed who I am today, my relationships with my children have done the same. Motherhood does things to your mind. My friend Molly agrees. "My kids are driving me crazy," she wails. That's not the kind of mind-altering experience we're talking about here. We're talking about being able to re-experience some of our own early childhood experiences once again as we either recreate or substantially alter them for our own children. Men don't enjoy this advantage. Their memory of how they were mothered is usually untouched by any experiences in their adult lives. Women, on the other hand, are constantly measuring and comparing their own childhood experiences with what is happening with their own children. And this is dramatically true when it comes to the mother-daughter relationship. There are, of course, many discrepancies between the way things were and the way we remember them. Our tendency to paint our experiences in either the best of colors or the bleakest of grays and blacks misses the obvious complexity of any mother-child relationship.

I have only recently had the opportunity to compare notes with my sister, ten years my junior. In some cases, our perceptions are very different.

> You couldn't control which, out of a day's events, would lodge themselves in your child's memory, to apply to her life and maybe alter the course of it. That was one of the most frightening aspects of being a parent: you never knew what a child was going to remember or how she was going to remember it.—Gail Godwin, *A Mother and Two Daughters*

The constant replay of our own childhood as we parent takes place in the context of trying either to duplicate the best or to drastically alter what we perceived to have been bad. This process changes us dramatically along the way. Our human frailties are exposed, our character flaws are magnified, and our opportunities for growth are enormous.

How Does Motherhood Change the Relationship We Have with Our Own Mothers?

"Pregnancy is a powerful stimulus for a daughter to examine her relationship with her own mother because she is now moving into her mother's shoes in a way she never did before," says psychiatrist Karen Johnson, M.D.

❦

"In many ways," continues Johnson, "this generation of women have lived very different from their mothers' lives, especially professionally. But the core expectations of motherhood haven't really changed. So when a woman moves into the stages of pregnancy and motherhood, she shares a similar role with her mother. The experience of taking on this new role not only transforms her life but gives her a chance to reexamine, rework, and sometimes repair her relationship with her own mother."[1]

Becoming a mother enables a woman to finally begin to understand what has happened between her and her mother and to begin making comparisons between how she thinks mothering should be and how her "inner computer" has been programmed.

As we talked together about how we redefine our own sense of self, Valerie, an editor and mother of two elementary-age daughters, points out a small but significant example of this in her own life. "When I was growing up, my mother was always interrupting my life and expecting me to jump," she shared. "Just when I was in the middle of something like a good book or a project she'd call me and expect an instant response. I would never do that to my daughters. I want to give them a sense that what they're doing is important." Although one small example, it is representative of the countless inner conversations women have with themselves as they mother their daughters.

How Is Mothering a Daughter Different from Mothering a Son?

I have both a daughter and a son. The psychology of my relationship with each of them is very different. I worry about my daughter's future with greater intensity. I feel the pain that she goes through more vividly than I do that of my son. While I love Patrick deeply and admire him intensely, I don't feel the need to protect him as I do my daughter. He is a separate person. But when I look at my daughter I see myself. I want her to avoid the mistakes I made and to shine where I didn't. Psychologists have put labels on these characteristics of the mother-daughter relationship that distinguish it from those we have with our sons: *identification* and *projection.* First of all we *identify* with our daughters. We envision them doing the things we have done but doing them better. As one woman put it, "I'm living my life vicariously through my daughter."

Secondly, we *project* on daughters our own feelings and attitudes about being a woman and a mother. If we've been unhappy in love and have endured a painful divorce, we project our suspicion and bitterness about men into our daughters' relationships. If we feel uncertain and lack self-confidence, these feelings will be translated into how our daughters perceive themselves. The women surveyed gave ample evidence of how the vicious cycle of self-doubt and low self-esteem is transmitted from generation to generation. Twelve of the eighty-eight women are caught in the middle between abusive or semi-abusive mothers and feelings of dissatisfaction and/or estrangement with their own daughters.

> What mother sings to the cradle
> goes all the way down to the coffin.
> —Henry Ward Beecher

Are We Destined to Become Our Mothers?

Psychologists tell us that while all significant adults in a child's life act as role models, their same-sex parent is the most powerful role model for a child. We learn how to act and behave in the world from watching our mothers. Wanting to know how the women of the study perceived themselves as being different from their mothers, I asked the question: "In what way(s) are you most different from your mother?"

Interesting enough, only one of the eighty-eight said she was like her mother in any way: "Internally I'm just as vulnerable as she is." One woman very surprisingly didn't know whether she was different or not. But the remaining women who answered the question were voluble in their remarks. While this group of women, as indicated earlier, do not consider themselves "feminists" or "liberated," the most frequent differences cited between themselves and their mothers was that they are more independent, assertive, competent, ambitious, and educated. The participants didn't think of themselves as liberated, but their answers to this question indicate that they are. They feel they are better communicators and more in touch with relationships and feelings than their mothers. They are more willing to talk about problems and confront issues.

Very few chose to view themselves in a less favorable light when compared to their mothers. One exception viewed herself as "not as smart, hardworking, or ambitious." But almost all of the other women felt that they'd been able to correct the mistakes that their mothers made, not only in marriages, but in relationships with their daughters.

I communicate in a more positive way with my children and accept them as individuals.

I'm more sensitive to the needs of my daughter and a much better communicator.

❦

I try to support and encourage rather than criticize and demean.

I give my children more emotional and spiritual support and keep communication open.

I hope I'm not as bitter, petty, and small.

I'm more open, understanding, and tolerant of my daughters.

Even one of the most traditional stay-at-home mothers who earlier had railed against the detrimental effects of the women's movement responded to the question this way: "I'm more outgoing and more able to make decisions on my own without asking my husband." If mothers are the powerful role models that theorists would have us believe, then the mothers of our respondents were either much different role models than their daughters perceive, or many other factors such as fathers, husbands, significant others, education, life experiences, and societal influences have combined to produce women who *perceive* that they are significantly different from their mothers.

My own life experiences confirm this. I've never really been able to figure out how my mother and I were connected. That is one of the reasons I am writing this book. We seemed close enough when I was in high school. We shared conversation over our daily breakfasts together, and she doted on my musical achievements and academic awards. She drove me to piano lessons on a weekly basis and pushed me to practice. One of my only memories of our doing something meaningful together as a twosome happened in high school. We signed up for a class at a weight-reducing salon and punished our bodies twice a week with machines and weights. She helped me study vocabulary for the SAT test while the machines massaged our thighs and we indulged in bags of caramel corn afterwards, telling ourselves we deserved it after all the hard work. But I never really told her what I was thinking and feeling. I don't know whether I felt she wasn't interested or wouldn't understand. I'm sure now that it was neither. She didn't know how to ask and didn't want to risk rejection, and I, too, sensed the possibility of the same. I was a solitary person lost in my own world of dreams, influenced deeply by the constant reading that consumed my life. I was eager to leave home and become my own person. Once I tasted college life in the exciting metropolitan Chicago area, I never returned for more than a couple of summer vacations and occasional brief visits. My choice of a mate did not meet my mother's expectations, and her lack of warmth and acceptance of the love of my life seemed to further push us apart. When my father died before the birth of my first child, there seemed to be nothing left to keep us together. What had masqueraded as a mother-daughter relationship dissolved when the anchor—my father—was gone. We visited with the children after she remarried, but there was always a strain; it never felt real. We were pretending to be mother and daughter. We never made it beyond formalities. There have always been significant women in my life—two wonderful aunts, always an older woman or two to serve as surrogate mothers and grandmothers, and scores of women friends, many of whom have participated in this study. Perhaps I was always looking for another mother.

I search for similarities between my mother and myself and can find only a few. I have become her antithesis and have only just begun to see how healthy and wonderful that is. I need not bathe myself in guilt because I am different than she is. I need not regret that I separated myself to live my own life. I believe we are not as bound by our mothers as the literature says. The respondents of the

❦

study are evidence of this. We are individuals with the power to change our own lives through our faith, our relationships, and the challenges that face each of us.

& Women who fulfill their vocation hold power even over powerful men; such women mold public opinion and prepare future generations. And so it is they who hold the power to save people from all our present and impending evils. Yes, women, mothers, in your hands more than in those of anyone else, lies the salvation of the world.—**Leo Tolstoy,** *The Lion and the Honeycomb*

CHAPTER THREE

Mothers and Young Daughters

*Our children—even when smeared with mud or misdeeds—
are God's gracious gift to us.*
DAVID GRANT, "A Grace Assignment,"
in *Christian Parenting Today*

EMILY WAS ONLY THREE. HER AFTERNOON NAP HAD STRETCHED far beyond its usual hour and the stillness from her room bespoke trouble. I quietly opened the door. She was deeply engrossed in what she was doing and didn't hear me enter. I stood motionless and watched. She was bent over her bedside lamp, decorating its shade with magic markers. I was at once horrified and amazed. Horrified at the destruction of my decorator lamp and amazed at the complexity and uniformity of the designs. I cleared my throat and she jumped, her big brown eyes wide with surprise.

As is frequently the case when confronted with misbehavior, I asked why. "Why are you drawing on the lamp?" I inquired.

"Because," she solemnly answered, "it's so dull."

Emily could not tolerate dull—not in her clothing, her friends, or her play. She wanted color, uniqueness, and individuality. While I was verbally reprimanding her for defacing the pristine whiteness of the shade, a part of me was applauding her spirit and creativity, her sense of adventure and certainty about what she was doing. I began to like this young daughter of mine in a new way on that particular day. I began to recognize that she was going to be much more than just her mother's daughter. She was becoming a person in her own right.

> ❧ God superintended your child's construction even down to the tips of her fingers. And just as surely as that child has her very own fingerprints, she has a lot of her very own other things as well— personality, perspective, and problems. She is as special as her fingerprints.—**Cliff Schimmels, *Oh No! Maybe My Child Is Normal!***

In the rest of this chapter we'll talk about mothering young daughters, our hopes and fears for the future, and the biggest challenges we face.

Four Views of the Mother-Daughter Relationship

The early years of mothering are a timeframe when the critical parenting foundations are laid—when mothers have the opportunity to change how they mother from how they were mothered. According to author Elizabeth Fishel, their choices fall into four categories.[1] They can choose to be *Traditionalists* who admire the way in which they were mothered and choose to replicate it with their own daughters. They can choose to be *Rebels* who parent in exactly the opposite fashion from the way they were parented. They can choose to be *Compensators* who are going to make up for everything in their daughters' lives that they lacked. Or they can choose to be *Synthesizers* who choose the best from the past and modify and change what should not be repeated. The mothers of this study are doing all four.

The Traditionalist

Paula is a Traditionalist. This thirty-three-year-old mother of two daughters resigned from her full-time job after the birth of her first child and is committed to being a stay-at-home mom. She and her mother enjoy a close and loving relationship. Paula describes her mother in this way:

> She is an extremely loving and giving person. She would do anything for her friends and family. She is my best friend and I can talk to her about everything!

The warmth and affirmation that Paula receives from her mother flows through to her daughters, ages three and five. Paula describes them this way:

> They have great personalities. One is very outgoing, kind to everyone and a real lover of people, animals and nature. My other daughter is more reserved, but funny and a real sweety.

Paula is delighted with the way she has been mothered and is following in her own mother's footsteps.

The Rebel

Tina is a Rebel. She is in conflict in both her marriage and her relationship with her mother. In both cases, the source of conflict is Dad. She and her husband disagree on all of the major issues of child

care, especially discipline. Tina doesn't agree with anything her
father does either. She is attempting to raise her daughters in the
midst of this conflict, and her frustration is only compounded by the
health problems of her children.

The Compensator

Cindy is a Compensator. Her mother is always angry and expects too
much of her. She treated Cindy like a peer during her growing-up
years, and through confrontation and counseling Cindy is beginning
to establish healthier boundaries. She wants to give her children
what she never had. Her desires can be seen in the tribute she wrote
to her three daughters, ages 6, 3, and 2:

> You are so young,
> but I pray from the depths of my heart
> that you will always know that
> NO MATTER what you do in your lives
> you are loved;
> NO MATTER how you may fail
> you are loved;
> NO MATTER what choices you make
> you are loved.

The Synthesizers

Many women are Synthesizers. They recognize areas of their own
parenting skills that need improvement and work diligently to overcome what they perceive as mistakes their own mothers made. "I'm
trying to communicate more directly and be less critical than my
mother was," said Amy. "But in her heart she is unselfish and generous. No matter what's happened between us, I've always known
she loved me, even when we're fighting."

❧

THE PURGATORY OF LOVING

Tonight
I hold my daughter at her window
while we trace the heat of sunset
colored like her chapped cheeks.
She rubs hers against mine
to cool them
to weave herself into me
to keep me in the room
and put off sleep.

Downstairs, my mother sleeps.
I have grown too large for her arms
too wise to risk words on.
She has diminished some.
I seem to look down
shrink back
wanting to have hatched from an egg.

I am in the purgatory of loving
between my mother and my child.
We move up the rungs
into lesser loving as we grow,
and my daughter
who hangs now
from my elbows
will stand behind me
on the second from the top rung
and want desperately
to push.
Judith Steinbergh

Most mothers of young daughters want to be more open with their daughters about sex than their mothers were with them. Kathy is emphasizing the emotional and psychological aspects of sex with her five-year-old rather than focusing on the cold scientific facts her mother gave her.

I'm trying to be open with her by telling her that when she was growing inside of me, I was so happy to feel her little arm move across my stomach.

Trish's discussions with her mother were in the form of warnings rather than information. Now she's reading books together with her daughters and is not embarrassed or uncomfortable about answering their questions.

What Are the Differences between Mothering a Young Daughter and a Young Son?

TRADITIONAL NURSERY RHYME

What are little boys made of?
Snips and snails and puppy-dog tails;
that's what little boys are made of.

What are little girls made of?
Sugar and spice and everything nice;
that's what little girls are made of.
Mother Goose

While many of the mothers of young daughters desired independence, self-actualization, successful careers, confidence, and healthy self-images for their offspring, there is research that suggests daughters are often treated in a much different way by their mothers than are sons. One study indicated that at three weeks of age, males were attended to, stimulated, imitated, and received affectionate contact from their mothers for twenty-seven minutes more per eight hours than females. Since infants slept from 25-75% of the time during the test periods, the increased time available for learning experiences for males was significant.[2]

Female babies frequently are not given as much parental encouragement as boys in their early strivings for independence and, consequently, do not develop the confidence and independence needed to cope with their environments.[3] Perhaps it is because we treat girls so differently from boys that in many cases women have a high need for belonging and approval that blocks their achievement motivation. As they raise young daughters, mothers must be sensitive to the subtle messages they can send daughters about their place in society.

TO MY FOUR-YEAR-OLD DAUGHTER

I lost my temper twice today,
Once when you ordered me around like a maid,
And once when you picked all the unripe plums
    from our tree.
You said I yelled so much it made you sleepy,
Popped in your thumb and drifted away.
Then, imagining you sad, I felt guilty.
You my firstborn child, my beautiful girl.
Remember when your ear hurt and we rocked all night,

How many hours, awake, I stared in your face
Seeing prongs that reach
Deep in your childhood, deep in mine.
Gail Todd, *Tangled Vines*

What Are the Biggest Conflicts between Mothers and Young Daughters?

Of the forty-two women surveyed who had young daughters, forty of them (95%) indicated an outstanding relationship. In the golden years between birth and age twelve, relationships are rosy for the most part. Problems are minor ones like hair, clothing, bedtime, completed chores, and an occasional cross word or temper tantrum. Personality clashes are less damaging and not long lasting. Overall, mothers of young daughters feel confident about their ability to handle almost any problem because their relationships with their children are strong.

As you will see in the next chapter, however, rocky times are ahead. As adolescence sets in, the love affair is over.

Will Working Full-Time Hurt a Young Daughter's Development?

Of those I surveyed, nine of the nineteen mothers of young daughters are stay-at-home moms. The remaining ten work—six at full-time professional careers and four at part-time writing, editing, or design-ing. Those who work have no regrets. They share responsibilities with their husbands and have enough financial resources to purchase reliable child care. While the controversy rages as to the damage done to children by working mothers, there is research to support some positive aspects to having a working mom, particularly for elementary-school-age daughters. One study showed that daughters of working mothers do not see the working mother as a threat to family happiness. They see work as something they will want to do when they are mothers.[4]

If mothers are not feeling guilty, fatigued, frustrated, and over-worked as a result of their dual responsibilities (only a portion of the reasons why many women can choose not to work), there are a number of important benefits that accrue to daughters of working moms: working mothers are often happier because their needs for self-fulfillment are being met; working mothers raise children who are independent and self-motivated; and working mothers normally don't have as much time to meddle and get over-involved in their children's day-to-day problems.

Whether or not you should work outside the home is up to you—not to your friends, your church, or "the experts." Each family works differently because it is made up of unique members. Evaluate care-fully your personality, your needs, and your family's needs before jumping to any conclusions. There are many options available to you.

What Worries Mothers of Young Daughters Most about Their Daughters' Futures?

Mothers of young daughters see the world as a very different place from when they were growing up. In many cases, they are deeply worried about the dangers that their daughters will face as they grow to maturity. They are worried about rape, AIDS, drugs, sex, the wrong peer groups, pain, and evil. Other mothers worry about their daughters' health and their ability to cope with disabilities. Raising young daughters today is not as easy as it once was. But it's not impossible either.

What Do Mothers of Young Daughters Hope for Their Futures?

Mothers of young daughters seem to be more concerned about their daughters' relationships with God than about any other facet of their lives. This is an understandable concern, since many young daughters have not reached the age of maturity to have a personal salvation experience.

> ❧ Oh, that our home on earth might be to them the pathway, the gate to the Father's home in heaven! Blessed Father, let us and our children be Thine wholly and forever. Amen.—**Andrew Murray, How to Raise Your Children for Christ**

In addition to wishes for a close Christian walk, mothers of young girls want positive self-images for their daughters. Along with the typical female characteristics of kindness, caring, sensitivity, and sweetness, mothers hope that their young daughters will focus their talents, step out in confidence as one of God's unique creations, and develop a strong sense of personal worth that will last them a lifetime.

For more information . . .

Chess, Stella and Jane Whitbread. *Daughters: From Infancy to Independence*. Garden City, N.Y.: Doubleday & Company, Inc., 1978.

Dunn, Rita and Kenneth Dunn. *How to Raise Independent and Professionally Successful Daughters.* Englewood Cliffs, N.J.: Prentice-Hall, Inc., 1977.

Powell, Barbara. *How to Raise a Successful Daughter.* Chicago: Nelson-Hall, 1979.

Rivers, Caryl, Rosalind Barnett, and Grace Baruch. *Beyond Sugar and Spice: How Women Grow, Learn, and Thrive.* New York: G.P. Putnam's Sons, 1979.

Zitzman, Susan M. *All-Day Care: Exploring the Options for You & Your Child.* Wheaton, Ill.: Harold Shaw Publishers, 1990.

CHAPTER FOUR

Mothers and Adolescent Daughters

*Children in a family are like flowers in a bouquet. There is
always one determined to face in an opposite direction
from the way the arranger desires.*
MARCELENE COX

SHE WANTED ME TO WEAR MORE JEWELRY, HANG UP MY
clothes, practice my piano lessons, and stop racing through life and
her house. I wanted her to worry less about what other people
thought, be more flexible, and stand up to her own mother once in a
while. She was the mother and I was the adolescent daughter. Our
differences seem minor in retrospect. I now wear more jewelry than I
should and hang up my clothes, but only on the weekends. I've
stopped playing the piano altogether, and I'm racing through life. I
still wish that she'd learned to care less about what other people
thought and stand up to her own mother—I think she would have
been happier and lived longer. My mother is dead now, but I wish

❦

she were here to read this book. I could tell her that I had a pretty terrific adolescence.

Such is not always the case. Ninety-one percent of the women who completed the questionnaire indicated a decline in the quality of their relationships with their own mothers when they reached adolescence. And the current relationships they have with their own daughters seem to be following the same rocky road. Ninety-five percent who have young daughters (birth to age 12) indicated outstanding relationships while only 24% of the women with adolescent daughters marked the outstanding category when asked to rate the relationships they had with their daughters. The quality of relationships begins to turn around as daughters move into young adulthood (38% indicated an outstanding relationship), and by the time daughters are in their late twenties, 49% indicated they enjoyed an outstanding relationship with their daughters.

What is there about this brief period in the mother-daughter relationship that generates so much distrust, hostility, argument, and estrangement between mothers and daughters? Is it inevitable? Does it serve some useful purpose in the developmental cycle? Or should we send our daughters away to live with surrogate mothers between the ages of thirteen and eighteen?

What Is Adolescence?

Different researchers and psychologists place different age parameters around the concept of adolescence. Some define it as the years between thirteen and seventeen. For me that definition starts too late and ends too early. For the purposes of this study, adolescence will be defined as that period from the ages of twelve to eighteen. Some precocious girls will begin exhibiting signs of adolescence as early as nine or ten, and many young women at the age of eighteen are

ൟ

scarcely ready to be considered young adults. But the "eye of the storm" of adolescence can most definitely be located between the ages of twelve and eighteen.

As mothers we have been set up for the problems we'll have with our daughters during adolescence. Gather a group of mothers of adolescent daughters together in one room and the collective angst of the group could defeat even the most competent psychologist or psychiatrist. We expect to have major problems and we get them. From Aristotle to Erik Erikson, we've consistently been led to believe that the norm for adolescence is bizarre behavior. We're almost embarrassed to confess to normality if such is the case in our household. But there are dozens of women who have only glowing things to say about their adolescent daughters. Life seems relatively smooth. A dynamic educator and mother of four, Marilyn described her twelve-year-old like this:

> I very much admire my daughter's intelligence and strength. At her young age she has the assurance and independence it has taken me most of my adult life to acquire.

Phyllis, a strong and confident woman who has worked since her daughter was two years of age, couldn't have been more positive when describing her about-to-be young-adult daughter:

> Many mothers threaten their daughters by saying "I hope you have a daughter someday just like yourself!" My prayer is that my daughter someday has a daughter as lovely, bright, and caring as she is. If she does, she'll be as blessed as I have been!

But there is ambivalence and dissatisfaction as many mothers describe their adolescents. Donna is a high-powered executive who

❦

commutes to the city by train early each morning. Her daughter doesn't share her drive for success.

> My daughter's role in our family appears to be that of one who doesn't succeed academically, and she puts forth no effort. She is a classic underachiever.

Another "successful" woman with two master's degrees who teaches at the university level is also disturbed by her daughter's lack of motivation.

> I want to push her to strive for levels she doesn't care about reaching.

Another mother bemoans the ups and downs of parenting an adolescent daughter.

> The worst part is trying to be patient when they do dumb things and you want to just tell them off or when they think they know it all and think you're from the Stone Age.

On the other hand, two researchers have questioned the conventional wisdom that describes every adolescent, either male or female, as a walking encyclopedia of psychological problems. Daniel Offer studied male adolescents (he was unable to procure money to study female adolescents at the time) and found that many young men survived the period with few, if any, problems. The subjects were stress-free, happy, and untroubled.[1] Giselle Konopka studied over two thousand adolescent girls and found that to a very high degree girls adhered to their parents' beliefs and valued their parents' views. Girls tended to choose friends with whom they felt they had values in common.[2]

❦

The picture seems not to be as bleak as one might believe. These studies are supported by the forty-two women in my study who had adolescent daughters. Only two of the group (5%) indicated a poor relationship with their adolescent daughters. The stories that Jamie and Kate had to tell were filled with despair and depression—alcoholism, anorexia, suicide, divorce, and abuse made up the fabric of their lives. Each was attempting to overcome a dysfunctional relationship with her own mother while picking up the pieces of a broken relationship with her adolescent daughter. They recognized the need for help and were using professional counselors to assist them. Clearly they represent the minority of mother-daughter relationships, but their lives cry out for healing and restoration. They demonstrate the power of dysfunction that can grip a family through generations.

Adolescence is an important developmental stage. Richard Lerner, a Penn State researcher, characterizes the period as one of "plasticity," suggesting that there is much opportunity for growth and change on the part of the individual.[3]

> God does not give bad gifts and good gifts; He simply gives different gifts. And when we can accept this in our children, we'll have come a long way toward understanding their uniqueness, and toward achieving family harmony.—**Jay Kesler,** *Ten Mistakes Parents Make with Teenagers*

Is There a Difference between Male and Female Adolescents?

Only recently have psychologists begun to look at female adolescence as a separate phenomenon. In the past many considered only a masculine model of human development. Erik Erikson, for example, theorized that male adolescents decided who they were and where they were going and in the process left their parents behind as they sought to define their independent selves. Erikson suggested that girls didn't go through this period. They waited, he said, until they met a husband who could help them achieve a true identity. Erikson assumed that in order to become an individual, adolescents—both male and female—must indeed separate from their parents.

But a healthier perspective on the needs of adolescent girls is set forth by Terri Apter in her book *Altered Loves: Mothers and Daughters During Adolescence*. She suggests that adolescents need to *transform* rather than *abandon* their relationships with their parents, and this is particularly true when examining the mother-daughter relationship. Daughters only separate, that is actually leave the relationship, if "the once nurturing love turns to strict confinement, only if they are unable to work within the relationships they so clearly value. Only then does an adolescent seek to break the childhood bond to the parent, only then is there an attempt to abandon the previous internal representations we all carry of our parents."[4]

Apter's theory is supported by the work of psychologists at both Harvard University and the University of Texas at Austin. But while male and female adolescents have the same needs for self-discovery and self-individuation, they clearly act out these needs in very different ways, particularly as they relate to mothers. Daughters desperately crave their mothers' approval, admiration, and affirmation. Even though adolescent daughters can be obstinate, argumentative, and hostile, they still want their mothers to love them unconditionally.

As mothers of adolescent daughters we have listened to their criticisms and complaints, all the while thinking that they merely wanted us to vanish and their lives would be complete. Apter suggests that the verbal parrying is an integral part of the adolescent attempt to get mother's validation of how she as the daughter is changing and maturing. Adolescent daughters want to be recognized and respected. They want to maintain their connectedness to us as mothers while continuing to get the recognition and acknowledgment that they are becoming adults. The girls in Apter's study said that the person they felt closest to, the person they felt most loved by, the person who offered them the greatest support, was their mother.[5]

What Are the Major Problems between Mothers and Daughters During Adolescence?

When one examines the issues that cause conflict between mothers and adolescent daughters, most of them are relatively unimportant. Mothers and adolescent daughters don't need something major in order to create an argument. They can do it over clothing, hair, food, housekeeping, or friends. Those are the problems that the women of the survey remembered from their own growing-up years. Today, with their own daughters, the problems haven't changed a whole lot. The list still contains food, friends, and housekeeping. New items that plague today's mother-daughter relationships are moodiness, lack of focus or goals in life, irresponsibility, and willfulness.

The real issues between mothers and adolescent daughters have to do with the process of girls finding their identity through relationships with others. Adolescent girls cannot begin to find their sense of self (a task that indeed can take a lifetime) without the "work" of talking through what is happening in their lives with an empathetic/ sympathetic ear. Who better should that individual be than Mother? My own daughter Emily and I have been hard at that work for the past year. Unfortunately for my budget, much of the work was completed via transatlantic or cross-country telephone lines. We have talked about life, death, premarital sex, marriage, love, commitment, and faith. From time to time during these often traumatic and emo-

❦

tional discussions, I would wonder if I had not given her enough guidance and support during adolescence to enable her to weather these storms on her own. After all, I reflected, I'd never "bothered" my mother with any of my problems when I was her age. It was only when I completed the research for this chapter that I achieved the "aha" that I hope will come to you as readers. Emily is smarter than I was. She recognizes that working through her problems with the help of an accepting, empathetic, and sympathetic ear will help her achieve her own sense of self and identity much more quickly and easily.

WHERE IS THE WEST

If my boundary stops here
I have daughters to draw new maps
    on the world
they will draw the lines of my face
they will draw with my gesture my voice
they will speak my words thinking they have
    invented them.

they will invent them
they will invent me
I will be planted again and again
I will wake in the eyes of their children's children
they will speak my words
**Ruth Whitman, *in the voice of pioneer woman
Tamsen Donner***

What Are the Joys of Parenting an Adolescent Daughter?

In spite of the frustrations and challenges of mothering an adolescent daughter, women are almost unanimous in finding the positives associated with this challenging task. Their positives fell into four main categories: 1. companionship and sharing; 2. achievement and independence; 3. spiritual maturity; and 4. sense of accomplishment as a mother.

Let's look at each of these categories.

Companionship and Sharing

Mothers of adolescent daughters enjoy spending time with their daughters. The mother of several adopted daughters put it this way:

> The best part of parenting an adolescent is when they just want to sit down and talk with you.

A former teacher who has spent more than the usual amount of hours with her adolescent daughter while home-schooling her said:

> Being able to talk and share ideas and thoughts is wonderful.

Some mothers worry about becoming too involved.

> My daughter shares much of her life and I have to be careful not to become too involved and to give her space. We've been very lucky in our relationship and we both really like each other.

Many mother-daughter pairs go out to lunch, swap clothes, and talk, talk, talk.

❦

Crystal, who was reared by her grandmother, finds she gets as much encouragement from her daughter as she gives. Her mother died when she was an infant, and the delights of discovering how much fun mothers and daughters can have together is a constant source of joy to her.

Achievement and independence

Mothers also revel in their daughters' independence and accomplishments. Many admit a vicarious thrill at seeing their daughters become more independent and assertive than they ever were. They admire the ambition, level-headedness, and achievements of their daughters. Pat, the mother of four daughters, put it this way:

> It's like watching butterflies emerge from cocoons.

"There are so many changes, and choices, and opportunities for my daughter," said Shirley, a college graduate who has been a full-time mom for over twenty years.

Spiritual maturity

A third area that brought satisfaction to mothers of adolescent daughters was their spiritual growth and maturity. "The thrill of seeing the love and prayers I've given for her begin to sprout when she makes a decision based on a concern for spiritual values is a tremendous thrill," shared Lee Ann, the single parent of two adopted daughters. "I've seen some of her friends being led to the Lord through her influences," said Betty, a Christian education director. "Seeing her grow in her trust for God is one of the best parts of parenting my daughter."

Sense of accomplishment as a mother

Finally, parenting adolescent girls, contrary to conventional wisdom, gives many mothers a sense of real accomplishment and affirmation of their skills as mothers. Diana, who runs her own decorating business, has four daughters. She says triumphantly:

> Watching them become assertive, independent, ambitious, and level-headed is tremendously rewarding. They are all girls I can be proud of.

What are the Frustrations of Parenting an Adolescent Daughter?

Adolescent girls are often rebellious, moody, outrageous, defiant, self-centered, and secretive. They think their mothers are stupid, close-minded, and intrusive (this according to their mothers). Only one of the women surveyed couldn't think of one single frustration in parenting an adolescent girl. Lucky woman! In addition to all of the above, mothers of adolescent girls spend a fair amount of time sharing the hurts, both real and imagined, that accompany their daughters' troubled voyages through the seas of adolescence. Julie put it this way:

> Having to stand by and watch her fail in her endeavors or see her get hurt by friends is really painful to me.

Another mother lamented:

> I'm powerless to change things for her. I have to let her experience some things for herself and have her own life.

❦

When I was an elementary school principal I received a telephone call late one evening. The caller, a mother of a twelve-year-old, wondered if I was aware of the problem in sixth grade. Alarmed, I envisioned drugs and sex rampant in my school. With relief I heard her detail the problem of cliques among the sixth-grade girls. "Can't you make the other girls like Sarah?" she pleaded. I smiled to myself. Adolescence was just beginning for her. I couldn't insure friendships for my own child, and I certainly couldn't do it for hers. Bearing and sharing the pain that our children endure through these difficult years is one of the major frustrations of parenting adolescent girls.

In addition to worrying about their daughters' happiness, mothers of adolescents worry about safety and purity, sex and drugs, alcohol and fast cars. They know what a scary place the world can be. They also know that their advice is not always welcomed or heeded.

≈ Adolescence is the age at which children stop asking questions because they know all the answers. — **Jo Petty, *Apples of Gold***

What about Sex?

The mothers I interviewed almost universally criticized the introduction to the facts of life they received from their mothers. They, on the other hand, are discussing the topic openly and extensively with their teenage daughters. Unfortunately, I did not have access to their adolescent daughters with whom to check perceptions. Kristen Moore of Child Trends, Inc., found that daughters whose mothers communicate their own traditional views about sex are less likely to engage in premature intercourse.[6] Other studies have stressed that any increased communication about sex reduces the probability of early sex. Most of the adolescent girls that Ann Caron interviewed for her study did not want to talk with their mothers about sex.[7] But

❦

Caron has some excellent tips for mothers of adolescent daughters who deal with this sensitive topic. She advises moms to examine their own sexual values and personal feelings about sexuality.

Communicate your sexual values and family values to your daughter. I had a perfect opportunity to do just that when Emily was entering junior high. We'd had the requisite talk about how your body changes, and I'd stumbled through "how the sperm and the egg get together," but somehow I'd never communicated the really important messages about how I felt about premarital intercourse. Emily came home from school one day and asked me to get a book for her from the public library. The title was *Forever* by Judy Blume. The topic was premarital sex between high schoolers. I could have refused to find the book. It would have been easy to do, but instead I got her a copy. After she finished reading it we discussed the values espoused by the book, with which I heartily disagreed. It proved to be the springboard for several excellent mother-daughter heart-to-hearts.

When you talk with your adolescent, emphasize the positive aspects of human sexuality. Provide a positive role model of what love, loyalty, and commitment really mean. And then model it, as much as you can, in your own life.

❧ Values are not *taught* to our children, they are *caught* by them.
   —**Unknown**

Is There Hope for the Mother-Daughter Relationship in Adolescence?

Given the nature of the adolescent girl and the tasks she must accomplish in her life before becoming a mature woman, there are bound to be stormy aspects to adolescence. But the recognition that

❦

these storms can usually be weathered without shipwreck should comfort mothers. Catherine Cooper at the University of Texas found that if a mother has an underlying trust and belief in her daughter and has expressed this belief with love and affection, the disagreements they have do not lead to hostility and avoidance. Successful mother-daughter pairs talk it out and do not view conflict as all bad. They disagree, negotiate, and learn to acknowledge one another's viewpoints.[8] We must find a way as mothers to bring our adolescent daughters to an understanding of the benefits of discussion, and we ourselves must cultivate the ability to deal with confrontation and conflict in a positive way. We must choose our "battles" wisely and not, as someone has said, "major on the minors."

Mothering Styles

In her parenting workshops, Ann Caron, the author of *Don't Stop Loving Me: A Reassuring Guide for Mothers of Adolescent Daughters*, uses a model of parenting developed by Earl S. Schaefer of the University of North Carolina.[9] It's the same model I use with my own children, and it's the model I encourage the teachers with whom I work to implement in their classrooms. There are four negative parenting styles in the Schaefer Circle: 1. accepting/non-demanding; 2. rejecting/detached; 3. accepting/control; and 4. rejecting/control. Each has its own pitfalls for the mother of an adolescent daughter.

Accepting/non-demanding
The accepting/non-demanding mother approaches parenting with a laissez-faire attitude. Marianne, whose daughter has declared herself to be a lesbian, seems to fall into that category. Marianne seems

❦

unalarmed by the sexual experimentation in which her daughter is engaging. Marianne supports and encourages her daughter. One would describe her as a loving parent. She just doesn't feel any sense of responsibility for her daughter's life.

Rejecting/detached

Also in the lax control half of the parenting circle is the rejecting/detached parenting style. Adolescents used to this kind of parenting style will go to any lengths to get their parents to notice them. Kate's adolescent daughter has run away from home, tried to commit suicide, and is now pregnant. She desperately wants to be noticed, and her efforts to achieve that notoriety are ruining her life. Kate seems powerless to stop her. She was parented by a rejecting/detached mother, and the cycle seems destined to repeat itself.

Accepting/control

The flip side of the non-demanding mother is one who accepts her child and the resulting responsibility but keeps such a firm control on her daughter's life that she leaves her child virtually defenseless when she gets out into the real world. The controlling mother must be informed of even the smallest detail in her daughter's life and loves to send her daughter on at least one or two guilt trips every day.

Rejecting/control

The fourth type of mother practices the rejecting/control style of parenting. The punitive, authoritarian parent falls into this category. These mothers resort to extensive verbal abuse and sometimes even physical abuse in an effort to control what they perceive to be their wayward adolescent daughters.

❦

Democratic parenting

None of the four parenting styles above will result in the type of nurturing, growth-evoking relationship that every mother wants with her daughter.

Schaefer posits that the best parenting is in the center of the accepting half of the circle and halfway between lax control and firm control. He calls it *democratic parenting*. Democratic parenting is not permissive, as some would believe. There is a lot of discussion and give and take. Opinions are invited and validated, but Mom gets the final say. The democratic parenting style nurtures a healthy respect between mother and daughter.

How Can I Successfully Mother an Adolescent Daughter?

How can you weather those adolescent years together successfully? Caron sets forth a number of other excellent principles to guide mother-daughter relationships through adolescence. They happen also to make good sense for parenting children of *any* age, and you can use them with sons as well.

Maintain respect for yourself as a woman and your role as a mother.

Somehow you will need to find a way to feel good about yourself, your accomplishments, and your role as a mother. Women who have deep unresolved conflicts with their own mothers, feelings of inferiority about their roles as wives and mothers, and the sense that life has passed them by have a difficult time parenting their daughters. They tend to become overinvolved in the lives of their daughters, caught in their daughters' emotional ups and downs in an unhealthy way.

❦

Be available.

Successful mothers of adolescent daughters find ways to be available to their daughters. They are always "there" or perhaps just a telephone call away. Although I worked throughout my daughter's schooling, she always had my telephone number tucked in her book bag. And she called often after school, just to see if I was there. Sometimes she was jubilant—sometimes down in the dumps. My role was to listen. She even called today while I was writing this chapter—from London, England. She sounded a little homesick. She'd been traveling through the United Kingdom on her own. In my day when I traveled with three friends it seemed a daunting task. I never could have attempted it alone. She learned some things about herself in the process, but she definitely needed to touch base with Mom just to reassure herself that I missed her and was suitably impressed with her accomplishments. I'm so glad that I happened to be at the other end of the phone on this sunny September afternoon.

Acknowledge your daughter's friends. Be friendly without being overbearing.

It's important when your daughter brings her friends home to strike just the right balance between acknowledgment and over-bearance. She doesn't want you to ignore her friends (either male or female), but neither does she want you to begin giving them the third degree or pull up a chair and join in the fun. Most daughters don't even mind if their mothers look fairly motherly. They find that preferable to competing with a mother who's trying to look like a teenager, too.

Remain firm when the issues are of importance to your family values.

There are many subjects that cause conflict between mothers and daughters that are of relative unimportance in the grand scheme of things—like how often your daughter's room gets cleaned or how short her skirt is. If you can jointly agree with your daughter on which issues she has control over, life with your adolescent will be happier. I generally left Emily's room up to her. She is an artist, collector, seamstress, and avid reader. As a teenager, and even now as a young adult her 9 x 12 room is a minefield of artist supplies, stacks of books and files, and assorted memorabilia collected on her travels. I've agreed that as long as the mess stays within the confines of her four walls, I will not impose my need for order and cleanliness upon her. We did, however, agree that her curfew was not a matter for debate. Although I trusted her implicitly, I felt the dangers on the highway multiplied tenfold after midnight. That is just one example of guidelines we reached together. While you can be somewhat flexible about some issues, when your family's basic values are under attack it's time to draw the line and take a firm stance. Your daughter wants you to draw the line. She doesn't want complete freedom. She needs the connections and anchor that her family supplies.

Maintain consistently high expectations for your daughter.

Let your daughter know that you believe in her ability to do whatever she sets her mind to. Encourage and support her in taking risks, and be ready to catch her when she falls. In the next section we'll explore what mothers of adolescent daughters most want for their futures.

❦

Exhibit confidence and pride in your daughter.

As I read through the forty-two questionnaires that mothers of adolescent daughters completed for this study, I know which mothers I'd like to have for my very own. They were the ones whose buttons seemed to burst with pride over the young women they were raising. They were amazed at their independence. They were delighted with their accomplishments. And they glowed with pride.

What Do Mothers Hope for Their Daughters' Futures?

Mothers of adolescent daughters want everything for their daughters as they grow to maturity—health, happiness, a strong faith, great careers, self-fulfillment, good marriages, and an integration of femininity with talents—everything they didn't have. These mothers are clearly caught in the middle. They've experienced some difficulty coming to grips with their lack of opportunities to "have it all." They want their daughters' lives to be different. One can imagine the wistful expressions and far-off stares as they reflect on unfulfilled expectations and shattered dreams: "I wish that my daughter will always have enough money to pay the bills," said a pastor's wife. A mother of three whose own family structure disintegrated when her father died and her mother remarried while she was still an adolescent said, "I hope that my daughters will have the freedom to make choices without the limits and constraints that I always felt."

"I hope that having a career won't preclude marriage as it did for me," shared Lina, whose two adopted multi-racial daughters have enriched her single life.

"I hope that she'll find men to date who are truly able to love," stated Ellen, whose first marriage ended in divorce.

❧

"I hope my daughter doesn't marry before she has a chance to live on her own. I hope she gets to know herself better than I did before marriage," lamented Grace, a middle-aged shop owner.

"I want my daughters to have the self-esteem and confidence to be all that they can be," said a stay-at-home mom who has not used her master's degree in public health since before her children were born.

"I lived with guilt for years before I came to Jesus. I want my daughter to be free from condemnation and self-hatred," shared Karen, who recently received her master's degree and is doing consulting work.

What do I, the author of this book, wish for my daughter Emily that I did not have? I hope that she will be able to continue the close and loving relationship she has had thus far with her mother. I hope that her mother, this author, will not repeat the mistakes of the past and close doors on relationships out of hardness of heart and bitterness, out of self-centeredness and stiff-necked pride. I hope that her mother, this author, has grown enough as a person to be a better mother than she was a daughter.

For more information . . .

There are a number of excellent resources that can help you understand your adolescent daughter and do a more effective job of parenting her.

Apter, Terri E. *Altered Loves: Mothers and Daughters During Adolescence.* New York: St. Martin's Press, 1990.

Caron, Ann F. *"Don't Stop Loving Me" : A Reassuring Guide for Mothers of Adolescent Daughters.* New York: Henry Holt and Company, 1990.

Chapian, Marie. *Mothers and Daughters: Learning to Be Friends.* Minneapolis: Bethany House Publishers, 1988.

Powell, Barbara. *How to Raise a Successful Daughter.* Chicago: Nelson-Hall, 1979.

Strom, Kay & Lisa. *Mothers and Daughters: Together We Can Work It Out.* Grand Rapids, Mich.: Baker Book House, 1988.

❧

CHAPTER FIVE

Mothers and Young Adult Daughters

What a happy day it was when you were born. And yet I did
not understand that day what happiness daughters can
bring. Collectively I love each of you for who you are.
You all are blessed with many different gifts but you
all are so loving to me and each other.
MOTHER OF THREE YOUNG ADULT DAUGHTERS

IT WAS DIFFICULT, IF NOT IMPOSSIBLE, TO WALK THROUGH HER
bedroom and the "stuff" that had spilled out into the hallway and
beyond. We were both tense, Emily and I. She was about to leave
home and begin college. I was about to "cut the cord." Both of us
were uncertain about the future. I knew *she* would be successful in
college; it was my own ability to face the day with equanimity that I
doubted. She knew I'd manage fine at home—my life is filled with
more challenge and excitement than any woman deserves. She was
worried about living with a strange roommate. As we crammed
boxes into the car at midnight in preparation for an early departure, I

remembered the day I'd left home. I hugged her and apologized for my impatience at her seeming procrastination. She had been on the phone with friends and saying good-bye to still others who stopped by. I could only think about finishing; she was saying good-bye to a whole part of her life.

FOR MY DAUGHTER'S TWENTY-FIRST BIRTHDAY

I stroked her cheek with my finger
and she began to suck for dear life
like a fish in the last stages of suffocation above water.
When I poured my voice down to revive her
she grinned and graduated from college
Summa Cum Laude, schools of minnows parting
    before her.

"You are not a fish," I said to her.
"You are my daughter, and just born, too.
You should know your place.
At least we are going to start off right."
Like a woman whose hand has just been severed
    at the wrist
but who can still feel pain winking in the lost finger,
I felt my stomach turn when she moved in her crib
    of seaweeds.
"Last month at this time," I said,
"you and my heart swam together like a pair of
    mackerel."

But she waved goodbye from a moving car,
hanging onto her straw hat with one hand,
light reflecting from the car window
as from an opened geode.
I wonder if she knows how I have stood for years
staring down through the fathoms between us
where her new body swims, paying out silver light.
Jeanne Murray Walker

What Is Young Adulthood?

Young adulthood is not as clearly defined an age period in the literature as is adolescence. Indeed, some experts stretch adolescence to include the college years. But the enormous differences between the personality and behaviors of a junior-high/early-high school student and a college student made me decide to look at young adulthood as a separate entity. So this definition of young adulthood is mine: *the period of time when a daughter leaves home for either college or to live on her own, roughly the ages between nineteen and twenty-three.* Daughters in this age group vary widely in their degree of independence. Their moods swing wildly from extraordinary competence to quivering masses of insecurities. They have many ideas about where they're going, but they've made no plans about how to get there. In the short space of four or five years, each of these young women will likely choose her life's mate, choose her life's work, and make decisions that will impact her life for decades. All of these impending choices are the stuff of which conflict is made in the lives of mothers and daughters.

What Are the Major Conflicts between Mothers and Young Adult Daughters?

As daughters begin to grapple with living as mature, separate adults, the conflicts between them and their mothers shift from the seemingly petty issues of clothing and music that created power struggles in adolescence to weightier problems like choice of mate, choice of church, choice of career, or choice of lifestyle. Young women of college age are still what many researchers call post-adolescents and are struggling to find the independence that has become an expectation in twentieth-century Western culture. Whether independence from parents is achieved through true separation from parents or by transferring dependence to another group or individual, the struggle can often be a stormy one.

In a study of one hundred autobiographical accounts of college women at Wellesley College, Sumru Erkut identified three types of mother-daughter relationships during the college years. Let's look at them.

Traditional
The first and smallest group is made up of young women who have been brought up in traditional households and expect to marry a man and raise a family. For this group of young women (about 10%), separation from their mothers (parents) is not accompanied by a search for independence. The mother-daughter relationship is smooth, with relatively few ups and downs.

Struggle for independence
The second group of young women (10-20% of the sample) do experience a struggle to become independent. But, as the author points out, "they manage to use their parents as role models and

sources of support, rather than seeing them as adversaries. They seem to come from families in which the parents had a strong bond. They showered their children with love but were not reluctant to set limits. In such families the mother-daughter (parent-child) relationship is often characterized as one of mutual love and respect." Allison's daughter is a perfect example of one who has survived the struggle for independence. She shared the following comments about her daughter:

> She has been a joy to me all of her life. My picture of her includes the sweet baby, the loving and obedient little girl, the fun and interesting adolescent, and the lovely, capable young woman she has become.

Open or silent conflict
The third group, close to 75% of the sample, held views of their mothers that were "unfavorable, judgmental, or otherwise unflattering." They were of two types: those who have open conflict with mothers and those who are "silent sufferers." Some daughters handled it through open warfare, while others sublimated their anger and insecurity under a relatively calm and obedient exterior.[1]

The findings of Sumru Erkut are supported in the stories of the mothers of young adult daughters who completed the questionnaire. Of this group of twenty-three women, seven are either divorced or in marriages that seem dysfunctional. Many of these same women also have less than ideal mother-daughter relationships. In one case, a young adult daughter has accused her father of sexual abuse, and her mother feels the charges are unbelievable and unsupported. Some of the women have grim views of marriage:

> I married someone like my father who worked all the time and was never home. Our family life centered around his work.

❦

You've got to stick it out no matter what, even if you're not happy or in love.

My mother and father thought marriage was permanent. I sure haven't passed that idea on to my daughter.

There is a strong temptation on the part of mothers trying to cope with troubled marriages to confide in their young adult daughters. Erkut points out the dangers involved:

It appears that in troubled marriages which continue, in separations and also in cases of divorce, a key factor in maintaining a positive mother-daughter relationship rests in mothers avoiding the temptation to treat their adolescent (young adult) daughter as a peer. If the daughter confides in the mother, that is quite appropriate. Providing advice, support and affirmation are among the primary roles parents play. The reverse of that situation, that is, the parent seeking advice, support, and affirmation from the adolescent however, is inappropriate. When the roles are reversed, the daughter not only loses her "mother figure" but she is simultaneously burdened by adult problems she did not create, can barely understand, and cannot solve.[2]

We cannot *press* our problems on our children just as they are learning how to solve their own problems. But as we share their realities and dreams and show our interest in their lives, without forcing ourselves on them, we will ease their transition into adulthood.

❧

What Would Mothers of Young Adult Daughters Do Differently?

A mother I had only just met was saying good-bye to her daughter—not just for the school term but forever. Her beautiful, bright, and energetic daughter, with a fresh college diploma, a brand-new job, and a shiny engagement ring was killed by a semi-trailer in a tragic automobile accident. Her mother and I were standing in front of an ornate coffin covered with funeral bouquets. Her college graduation picture stood nearby. I had worked with this young woman for four months. I felt like she was my daughter. She was a student teacher in the building where I was the principal. She was a remarkable person. I've seen dozens of student teachers come and go, but none that touched the lives of more students and teachers than Katharine. She was mature and caring, a sensitive Christian young woman with a real mission in life, to touch young lives. Her mother can be very proud of all she accomplished in her short life. She should have no regrets about Katherine's life at all, except that it was so painfully short.

As mothers travel the highway of parenting, there is little time for reflection when children are small. The demands of mothering are too great. But as our children face adulthood we begin to look at them more objectively. Our worries go far beyond wondering if they've remembered to look both ways before they cross the street:

- Will she be a successful adult who can manage on her own?
- Am I to blame for that little streak of irresponsibility?
- Will she choose the values and beliefs that I hold dear?

- Should I have sent her to a Christian school?
- Is the world of work ready for her unusual style of dress? Should I have been more demanding of her personal appearance?

      We strive to produce responsible adults who are able to function independently of parents' authority, yet wholly submitted to God's. If all goes well, they should become adults who live directly responsible to God within the limitations He has ordained.
— **Charles Stanley,** *How to Keep Your Kids on Your Team*

In those quiet moments the doubts come creeping in.

As mothers of young adults, we wish we'd spent more time with our daughters. Perhaps, as single parents, some of us did not enjoy the luxury of being "stay-at-home" moms. We want to turn back the clock and savor simple moments together as mother and daughter. Our daughters leave the nest too soon. We wish we had affirmed them more and been more willing to accept them the way they were. In spite of what we wish we could have had from our own mothers, many times we still don't provide those things for our own young adult daughters. One mother I surveyed regretted her lack of spiritual vision for her daughter:

> I would have exposed her more to church and religion when she was younger.

There was one mother who, in what could only have been a moment of sheer bliss, penned "nothing," when asked what she would have done differently. What a fortunate woman! I wish I could say the same.

❧

Perhaps we've indulged our daughters and wonder if we did the right thing.

I suspect her lack of responsibility is due to my eagerness to do everything for her.

I'd have given her fewer things.

I wish I'd gotten after her organizational skills and made her watch less T.V.

I wish I'd encouraged more independence and goal orientation.

Self-doubt is part of the baggage of being a mother. We'll always wonder if it's our fault. But as I grow older, I'm becoming less willing to blame my own mother. Along with that, I'm becoming less willing to take all of the responsibility for what my daughter will become, for I realize I'm only part of the picture. She is an individual, just like I am—and I must allow her to make her own choices.

What about Lifestyle Choices?

Perhaps the hardest thing to accept as a parent is seeing your daughter make a bad decision regarding her lifestyle. When our daughters begin to date young men, our anxiety about what will happen reaches new heights. And when they don't date, we get even more concerned. Two of the women surveyed indicated that their young adult daughters have chosen "alternative"—lesbian—lifestyles. Each mother responded differently to this choice. Joan, a businesswoman, is deeply disturbed at her daughter's choice of lifestyle. She has invited her daughter's companion to family activities and is trying hard to accept her relationship, but her child's sexual preference is a constant source of anguish to her. She also wonders what she did wrong in her parenting to "allow" this to happen.

Maxine, a "stay-at-home" mom, seems totally comfortable with her daughter as a lesbian. She stated that they discuss the subject frequently, and her daughter's militant participation in lesbian political movements and frequent sexual liaisons seem not to bother her.

The respondents have faced other lifestyle choices their daughters have made in addition to homosexuality. When Joyce's daughter came home from a college semester abroad, she told her mom tearfully that she had just had an abortion. Although torn apart inside from her daughter's actions, Joyce consistently and lovingly reaches out to her daughter, helping her deal with the aftermath of her abortion. Gwen is helping her young adult daughter overcome a serious eating disorder through therapy and family support. Still another is helping her young adult daughter through a painful divorce. Their pain becomes our pain, and their choices become ours in many cases. In Joyce's words: "I'm there to help whenever I'm needed."

But at the same time we are helping, we must remember that our daughters are in fact young adults. Throughout their growing up they have acquired more strength to face difficulties than we can imagine. They had the right to make their lifestyle choices. And now they will live with the consequences of those choices. It is not our place to "save" them from their actions (as if we *could*), but we can always be "there"—to listen and to give assistance, when it is needed, when it is welcomed.

❧

What Happens When Your Young Adult Daughter Isn't Really a Young Adult?

Those of us who are engrossed in the ever-changing lives of our young adult daughters seldom think about those mothers whose daughters are physically and mentally challenged. Nancy Doyle Chalfant is such a mother. She tells the story of Verlinda, her mentally retarded daughter in her book, *Child of Grace*.

A mother never quite forgets that once she carried her child within her. During the pregnancy her physical body was busy creating the physical body of her baby, while her mind and heart were creating plans and dreams about what the baby would be like, what she would do, and what a joy she would be to the rest of the family. A mother is full of hopes for the baby's physical health and wholeness, and she eagerly anticipates the addition of a new personality to the family circle. Although the thought of physical or mental disability might enter her mind during that time, she would most likely put it out of her thoughts before it had any reality to her.

But when those dreams and hopes are torn away, a mother faces despair; they were too much a part of her to dismiss easily. Many parents of handicapped children have gone through the experience of being reminded of smashed hopes. It often happens when we see a child who is the same age as ours. We look at the child and can hardly believe that he has made so much progress. We have begun to adjust to and accept our own child, then it hits us again with a force that is overwhelming. It can send us back to the beginning to face the same emotions and fears again.[3]

Chalfant relates her feelings upon seeing young adult men and women of her daughter Verlinda's age. We who have blissfully sailed through childbirth with scarcely a twinge are brought up short to face our own minor disappointments and frustrations with embarrassment and humility.

🔊 Unconditional love is loving a child no matter what. No matter what the child looks like. No matter what her assets, liabilities, handicaps. No matter what we expect her to be, and most difficult, no matter how she acts.—**Ross Campbell, How to Really Love Your Child**

Susan McGee Bailey, also the mother of a retarded young adult daughter, shared these comments at a Wellesley College colloqium on mothers and daughters.[4] After Bailey described her own relationship with her mother she continued:

I have been a mother for nineteen years, but my daughter cannot listen to reminiscences and weave a story. She cannot plan a life of adventure or of domesticity—or of some elaborate, delicious combination of both. Amy is both physically and mentally disabled, and it is difficult for her to finish a short children's story, let alone maintain an interest in events long past of which she was not a part, or dream dreams of days to come and the ways she will be in the world. Amy cannot be left alone for any length of time, so child care remains a pressing problem. She doesn't drive, so the "mother as taxi-cab" years go on and on. There are days when I long for a life that will not be totally structured around my daughter's needs.

Amy is 19. It is time for her to make plans to leave home, but leaving home is not something to be planned by Amy. Leaving home is not something which I as her mother try to subtly influence while she as my daughter guards against this influence with silences and secrets. Amy's leaving home is one more thing that I must arrange for her. I must help Amy to leave me with confidence and joy. For if she stays with me how can she learn those things I cannot teach her?

How Can I Successfully Mother a Young Adult Daughter?

The same rules that applied to the mother-daughter relationship in adolescence are applicable to mothering young adult daughters. One additional caution mentioned earlier bears repeating. As daughters mature, there is the temptation to think of them as peers rather than daughters. Sharing your marital problems or any other personal problems with your daughter will place her in the awkward position of confidante and will cause your daughter to lose her mother figure. In the words of one of Erkut's subjects:

During the worsening of their marital situation, my mother and I started to confide in each other. Through our talks, I learned a lot about the situation and the things my father did to make it worse. As these conversations continued, I heard much about the personal problems between my parents also. A closeness developed between my mother and myself—a closeness which had the potential for serious problems . . . I started having problems in school and sought the help of the school psychologist. Counseling brought out my anger towards my mother. I am mad at her for subjecting me to the problems between her and my father. Many of them are quite personal and not the type of things with which I as a daughter should have to deal. Somehow I felt it was my duty to listen to her which I know now it is not.[5]

❧

While my own young adult daughter and I have had dozens of conversations about her own despair and search for meaning since the death of her father, and while I have certainly let her know that I am hurting deeply as well, I never come to her when I am feeling in need of counsel and comfort. I go to my own adult friends who can relate to me as an adult. Confiding in my daughter that I feel as perilously close to the edge as she does will only serve to exacerbate her situation. She does not need to share my problems as she attempts to create meaning out of this terrible loss in her own life. It wouldn't be fair to her—or to me. And our relationship, one of the most precious things on earth to me, would suffer.

Brushing out my daughter's dark
silken hair before the mirror
I see the grey gleaming on my head,
the silver-haired servant behind her. Why is it
just as we begin to go
they begin to arrive, the fold in my neck
clarifying as the fine bones of her
hips sharpen? As my skin shows
its dry pitting, she opens
like a small pale flower on the tip of a cactus;
as my last chances to bear a child
are falling through my body, the duds among them,
her full purse of eggs, round and
firm as hard-boiled yolks, is about
to snap its clasp. I brush her tangled
fragrant hair at bedtime. It's an old
story—the oldest we have on our planet—
the story of replacement.
Sharon Olds

What Do Mothers of Young Adult Daughters Wish for Their Futures?

Mothers of young adult daughters want everything for their daughters: fulfillment, happiness, spiritual growth, a good career, a wonderful marriage, independence, self-esteem and, above all, avoidance of the mistakes that plagued their mothers' lives.

I hope she has more confidence in God and herself than I did.

I hope she'll be happier in her upcoming marriage than I've been.

I hope she'll get married before becoming pregnant.

I hope that she'll realize she's "enough." Smart enough, pretty enough, etc.

We as mothers want the best—of course!—for our daughters. We want them to succeed in every way—emotionally, spiritually, mentally, financially, and socially. We want them to feel like champions, not for our sakes, but for theirs. But most of all, we want them to know that, no matter what, we love them.

For more information . . .

Apter, Terri. *Altered Loves: Mothers and Daughters During Adolescence.* New York: St. Martin's Press, 1990.

Bence, Evelyn. *Leaving Home.* Wheaton, Ill.: Tyndale House, 1986.

Caron, Ann F. *Don't Stop Loving Me: A Reassuring Guide for Mothers of Adolescent Daughters.* New York: Holt, 1990.

CHAPTER SIX

Mothers and Adult Daughters

*The Lord couldn't have given me a better daughter. She has
been a continual source of pride, love, and wonder as she has
grown into such a sensitive, kind, godly woman. She is a
woman of deep commitment to Jesus Christ, a strong sense of
values, considerate of the feelings of others. She gives good
advice; her peers seek her out for guidance and counsel. I'm
proud of her. I learn from her. My daughter, my friend.*

CHERI

W<small>E TALK OFTEN TOGETHER OF MOTHERS AND DAUGHTERS, MY</small>
friend Marie and I. At our weekly breakfasts we've shared joys, but
have shed many tears together. She speaks of her daughter, a grown
woman now married. I speak of my mother, turning to dust in her
grave. She strives to understand her daughter's anger and distance. I
can't explain it to her. How can I when I still can't totally explain my
own estrangement from my mother? Are there similarities between

Marie's daughter and me? Perhaps. But each adult daughter and mother write their own story and each is unique.

I've read and re-read the eighty-eight questionnaires. They are spread out on my family-room floor, and I sort through them from time to time looking for that elusive piece of information I need. The women who completed them did so with an intensity I found surprising. It's not easy to bare your soul on paper. Some were doing it for a stranger and, possibly even more difficult, some were doing it for a friend. I have come to know and love these women for their honesty and to ache and rejoice with them for the complexity and richness of their lives. Nowhere is that complexity and richness seen more eloquently than in the relationships they have with their own adult daughters and mothers. Many are working through painful experiences with dignity and diligence. Many are enjoying the fruits of love's labor as they see their mothering expertise replicated in the homes and families of their daughters. And still others are in pain, trying to find out how they can make their mothers love them.

In this chapter we'll explore the complex world of mothers and adult daughters. For the first time, our perspective will be a dual one. Thus far, we've considered only the respondents' relationships with their own daughters—through the early years, adolescence, and finally as young adults. Now, we'll look at women who are both daughters and mothers—women in the middle. Such women, like myself, must find a way to handle both of these relationships, and therein lies the most challenging part of being a woman. Frequently we fight the same battle on both fronts—the battle for acceptance and affirmation. And even more often we are called upon for nurturing and support from both our mothers and our daughters. Once again, I will call upon the women who answered my questionnaire. We will look specifically at the twenty-nine women (ages 48-76) who have adult daughters (25-50), but at the same time we'll con-

❦

sider all eighty-eight women and the relationships they presently have with their own mothers.

The limitations of a study such as mine are never more evident than in this chapter. Without interviewing pairs of mothers and daughters simultaneously we have only one side of the story. However, the comfort and strength for me as an author comes from the sense that I am not alone—other women share my joys and other women share my pain. We are sisters in our shared experiences, and we can help each other.

What Do We Really Believe about Mothers and Daughters, and How Does It Affect the Way We Behave?

Well-known biographies such as *My Mother, Myself* and *Mommy Dearest* serve to reinforce the popular notion that mother-daughter relationships are almost always doomed to conflict and unhappiness. The eighty-eight women of this study do not feel that way about their mothers and daughters.

My mother always was and is an unconditional lover for me and did affirm my strengths. This provided me with confidence and a core of knowledge of who I am and what good "stuff" I'm made of. I will be forever grateful and pass this on to my own precious daughters. It is a personal treasure and the basis of what I can become.

One of the things that really impresses me about my mom is that even though she is very gifted, intelligent, and motivated, she put her children first while they were at home. She started her MBA before I was born but then put it on hold until my youngest brother was in college. Thirty years later she walked across that stage and we were all so proud. Not only because she accomplished it but because she

❦

did it without sacrificing us kids. We were her priority, and it paid off in the relationship we have today. Young women today should take note.

Another negative assumption is that the relationships are most conflictual if adult daughters have their own careers and families, i.e., if they're caught in the middle. All of the women in this study are in the middle, and whether they were stay-at-home moms or high-powered executives had no bearing on their mother-daughter relationships. A third mistaken assumption not supported by research is that mother-daughter relationships are more important than father-daughter relationships. The women who completed the study talked about their fathers frequently. Fathers were an important part of their relationships with their mothers and an important factor in their outlook on life. They cared deeply for their fathers.

Rosalind Barnett points out three additional factors that often inhibit adult daughters as they seek to relate to their mothers. The first has to do with the differences that exist between generations that conspire to keep us apart. Experiences with the issues of education, career, birth control, and divorce differ widely between generations. My own mother graduated from high school; I have a doctorate. My mother never worked outside of the home; I have a career. I used birth control for five years to plan my family; my mother got pregnant almost immediately after marriage and suffered through three miscarriages in addition to two more live births. My friends get divorced when marital differences become irreconcilable; my mother and her friends stay married no matter what. Given these differences, we as women sometimes, and perhaps rightfully so in some cases, assume our mothers are viewing our lives with critical eyes. They may not approve of our lifestyles, and we want their approval, but we also have a strong need to live our own lives.

❦

Consequently, we have a difficult time separating the choices we're making for ourselves and those we're making to please our mothers.

Barnett suggests a second factor that may serve to inhibit close adult mother-daughter relationships: the unspoken fears of what would really happen if we were honest and shared with our mothers or daughters what we truly want from each other. Adult daughters may worry that they'll be thought of as immature if they share too much with their mothers. Or daughters may worry that they'll open up a Pandora's box of mother-care if they become too close.

A third reason cited by Barnett is the tendency in our current society to blame Mom for everything. Mother-blame is rampant and does little to reinforce the basically positive nature of the majority of mother-daughter relationships. As we will see in the following section, Barnett's thesis that there are many forces at work conspiring to keep mothers and daughters apart has merit.

What Are the Major Conflicts between Mothers and Their Adult Daughters?

The serious conflicts between women and their daughters as they reach maturity seem to either disappear almost completely or solidify into serious estrangement. Thirty-eight percent of those who answered the questionnaire (thirty women) indicated an excellent relationship with their mothers, 49% (thirty-nine women) indicated an average relationship, while only 13% (ten women) indicated a poor relationship. Many of the respondents indicated no conflicts, and many others indicated a continually improving relationship.

We had the typical teenage conflicts, but there's nothing worth mentioning now.

❧

We're not crazy about her church preference but we really haven't had many conflicts.

My eldest daughter was very critical when she was going through a tough time in her life, but now those problems are all resolved and we have a good relationship.

In those relationships where conflict is major, divorce and/or remarriage of either the daughter or the mother is one of the major causes, followed closely by daughters choosing mates who are unacceptable to mothers (and fathers). Daughters are usually hurt and confused by the divorce of their parents and even more deeply resentful of their mothers' remarriages. They choose to estrange themselves from their mothers rather than cope with the new spouse. Conversely, mothers find it difficult to accept either marriage to an unacceptable mate for their daughters or divorce from son-in-laws to whom they've become attached. (Six percent of the daughters in the study have been divorced.)

A mother of three daughters shares her pain:

I suffer with grief over the poor first husband. I'm angry at being involved in a wedding for a marriage that didn't work out. I haven't related to the second husband in my feelings. He's of a different nationality and language, which makes it even more difficult.

A pastor's wife, now retired from her own professional career, also mourns the loss of her daughter's husband:

Some fellow-workers (of my daughter's) and a self-appointed guru brought about the divorce and change in her attitudes. We appreciated

❧

her husband, and he was appreciative. My daughter and I have been estranged over it.

Sometimes the reasons for estrangement aren't always evident to the respondents. That's when the pain is most severe.

I was estranged from my daughter when I divorced (she was in college), and now (she is 30 and married) we've had problems for about a year and a half. I've tried to work it out and couldn't so I'm just waiting it out. I've tried everything—books, counseling, ministers. Nothing has helped. I just wish my daughter would stop blaming me and hanging on to the past. I wish she'd accept me the way I am and begin having a relationship.

What Are the Major Conflicts between Adult Daughters and Their Mothers?

While 87% (sixty-nine women) felt they enjoyed an average to excellent relationship with their mothers, almost all of them had things they wished their mothers would start or stop doing. What the questionnaire did not always uncover was whether this request had been shared with their mothers or remained unspoken. Surprisingly, a major point of contention is fathers.

She can be very critical of other people, especially my father.

I can't stand how she caters to my father.

Her protection of my father by refusing to ever let confrontation surface drives me crazy.

❦

I wish she wouldn't take so much abuse from my father.

My mother waits on my father hand and foot.

Conversely, the daughters feel that their mothers are critical of their mates, how they keep house, and how they raise their children.

It took my mother fifteen years to accept the man I married.

She wasn't crazy about my choice of husband. She felt I was too young and he had too many flaws.

I keep a really messy house and this upsets my mother.

She feels I cater too much to my children which is amusing because she's the "queen" of catering.

While problems of housekeeping and childrearing are common bones of contention between mothers and daughters, they can easily be ignored or surmounted. No one ever needed counseling just because they didn't dust every week. More serious and alarming, however, were the significant number of women who seem to suffer serious problems with self-esteem and self-doubt because of the perceived or actual psychological abuse they received and are still receiving from their mothers.

She never seemed to approve of what I did or thought. She feels so unloved that she's always testing to see if you love her.

It wasn't enough to do the dishes. They had to be washed exactly the way my mother did it.

❧

My mother's lived with me for twenty-two years since my dad died, and she has to be always right and know more than me. She's always competed with me for control and authority in my life.

She gave me the feeling that I was never quite smart enough or good enough. She expressed her opinions often and loudly.

She has a violent and hateful temper. I can't stand her isolation and bitterness.

I can't act like a mature adult in her presence. Somehow I feel defensive when I'm around her.

The words of these respondents echo the feelings of Cohler and Grunebaum who, in writing about mother-daughter relationships in general, state that: "The relationship between adult women and their own mothers is perhaps the most complex and emotionally charged of all relationships within the family."[2] As in all relationships, the mother-daughter bond has much potential for good, or for hurt. Either can last a lifetime.

What Does the Mother-Daughter Relationship Do to Your Health?

Is there any connection between daughters' feelings of anxiety and depression and the quality of their relationships with their mothers and fathers? Rosalind Barnett found in a study of four hundred employed women aged 25-55 that if a daughter has a poor relationship with either her mother or father, her levels of anxiety and depression are high; if she has a good relationship, her levels of anxiety and depression are low. Daughters who have positive rela-

❧

tionships with their mothers report higher self-esteem, overall life satisfaction, happiness, and optimism than do daughters who report troubled relationships with their mothers.

> I thank God every day for the Christian legacy my mother gave me and I wish she'd written a book on her wisdom in raising her five children on a very modest income. The love she poured out to her children was beautiful and strong.

> I'm so fortunate to have come from an intact, loving family. Although Mom's not perfect she's never stopped loving me; for that I'm grateful.

Younger, single women and those without children need the relationships with their mothers even more for good mental health, however, since they do not have other roles to play as wives and mothers.[3]

The Death of Your Mother—What Will It Mean?

The majority of the women of this study (over sixty) will face the death of their mothers in the next twenty years. Twenty-one of the respondents' mothers are already deceased. Two lost mothers in infancy, two in childhood, eight in young adulthood, and two in middle-age. My own mother died in 1985. While losing a parent ranks as one of the most important and difficult emotional tasks of adult life, losing one's mother is even more complicated. While we're always Daddy's little girl in some sense, a large majority of women look upon their mothers also as peers. No matter how "good" or "bad" the mother-daughter relationship has been, the breaking of it through death will be painful and life-changing.

Conceived by your loving,
formed from your substance,
I sucked from you life-giving milk.

Rocked in your arms, lulled by your singing,
I mirrored your smiles, mimicked your phrases.

Sensing your joys and your unspoken anger,
I tested with you what a person could be.

Together we loosened the silver cord.
I gathered confidence, made my own journey.

Chose my own love, had my own daughters.
Watched them grow strong, let them go freely.

My arms push your chair, my eyes read your mail.
Your queries ask for my confirmation.

I drew from you strength for my living
Can you draw from me courage for dying?
Alice Johnston Brown

What Are the Main Types of Relationships between Adult Daughters and Their Mothers?

In her book, *Linked Lives: Adult Daughters and their Mothers,* Lucy Rose Fischer describes five types of mother-adult daughter relationships that she hypothesized based on in-depth interviews of forty-three pairs of mothers and daughters. These types are Responsible Mother/Dependent Daughter (Type I); Responsible Daughter/Dependent Mother (Type II); Peerlike Friendship (Type III); Mutual Mothering (Type IV); and Uninvolved (Type V).[4] While I did not enjoy the luxury of face-to-face interviews with matched pairs as did Fischer, I was nevertheless curious to know how the women of the study would characterize their relationships with their own mothers and similarly how the women who had adult daughters would describe those relationships. I gave them a brief description of the five types of mother-daughter relationships and asked them to rate their own (see Appendix B). The descriptions are as follows:

Type I: Responsible Mother/Dependent Daughter
In the Responsible Mother/Dependent Daughter, mothers cater to daughters' emotional and physical needs. This relationship would be the norm for mothers of very young and adolescent daughters.

Type II: Responsible Daughter/Dependent Mother
This type is characterized by daughters being more likely to give than to receive help from mothers. This relationship is often the norm for women with much older mothers.

Type III: Peerlike Friendship
In the Peerlike Friendship type, there is a high degree of involvement in each others' lives, but both mother and daughter maintain a great amount of autonomy and independence.

Type IV: Mutual Mothering
Mothers and daughters who engage in Mutual Mothering have a sense of mutual responsibility and protectiveness. There is much

❦

involvement in each others' activities, and they telephone or visit with each other daily.

Type V: Uninvolved
Mothers and daughters in this category have a complete lack of emotional involvement in each other's lives.

Fischer described eleven of her forty-three pairs as Responsible Mothers/Dependent Daughters. These relationships were characterized by mother's close supervision and control over an adult daughter, with the mother offering direction to her daughter's life, which is not surprising since the daughters in these eleven pairs were age twenty-five or younger. Three of the women in my study indicated having a Type I relationship with their mothers. In two cases the choice was based on a relationship they had enjoyed in the past (one mother was deceased and one surrogate mother has Alzheimers), and the contents of their questionnaires indicated a deep desire to reaffirm to themselves that their mothers did at one time cater to their emotional and physical needs. The third respondent was a thirty-two-year-old mother of two whose sixty-three-year-old mother lives in the same town and is very involved in her life. The respondent still feels very connected to both of her parents and they appear to meet many emotional and physical needs in her life. She appears to have "two homes."

None of the women who are mothers of adult daughters indicated having a Type I relationship with their daughters.

Eighteen of the respondents characterized the relationships they had with their mothers as Responsible Daughter/Dependent Mother. While for the majority of these women the care is physical because of aging mothers living either in their homes or in nursing homes, in many cases the emotional dependency is not age-related. A thirty-three-year-old mother of three daughters shares her experience:

> I had an unhealthy caretaking role with my mother in my growing-up years. I've stopped taking care of her now. She treated me like a peer when I should have been treated like a child. I've chosen to confront my past through counseling.

A fifty-four-year-old who is having problems with both her mother and her daughter sees her caretaking role as nothing new:

> I feel like I've taken care of my mother since I was eight years old.

Mutual mothering includes a constant switching back and forth between mothering and being mothered. These relationships are not always filled with harmony and consensus, but the conflict does not seem to interfere with the ties that bind.

Fischer's research indicated that genuine peerlike friendships between mothers and daughters are somewhat uncommon. Only six of her forty-three subjects approximated this relationship in Fischer's opinion. She describes it as one in which "both mother and daughter are careful not to exercise control over each other's lives."[5] While, once again, my subjects self-selected their type of relationship based on a very brief description of the types, the information they shared on the questionnaires about both their personal lives and their mother-daughter relationships gives evidence that this group is very independent. Nineteen women selected this type as characterizing the relationship they have with their mothers. A forty-four-year-old mother of two daughters talks about her own struggle for independence:

❦

I wish I could have become independent without as much pain to my mother and myself. However, without becoming independent, my mother and I would have had only pain today. She has grown to accept some differences of opinion, but she staunchly remains faithful to her own interests.

Catherine, a fifty-year-old music teacher whose only daughter recently married, enjoys peer relationships with both her mother and daughter.

My mother is very hardworking and very capable of doing anything she sets her mind on. She built a deck on the back of her house last year. She was seventy-four years old.

Catherine is also moving toward a peerlike relationship with her daughter.

We're more like friends now than mother and daughter. Now that she's a wife, I don't mother her as much.

Almost all of the mothers of adult daughters described their relationships with their daughters as Peerlike Friendships. Frances, the mother of several adult daughters, talked about the daughter who has most recently married:

Now that she's independent of me, I would advise her if asked, but she and her husband now make their own decisions.

Ten of the eighty-eight respondents characterized the relationships with their own mothers as Mutual Mothering, while nineteen

❦

selected Peerlike Friendship. Both Mutual Mothering and Peerlike Friendship are symmetrical relationships where mothers and daughters respond to each other in roughly equivalent ways. The primary difference between the two is the degree of independence for both the daughter and the mother.

The Mutual-Mothering relationship can be seen in the lives of Colette, age 33, and her mother, age 58. They have both been elementary-school teachers and are now stay-at-home moms. As Colette says:

> I talk to my mother almost every day even though she lives over fifty miles away. My folks visit often and we go to their house often. She shares her joys and concerns with me and I with her. We are always there for each other.

Six of Fischer's forty-three subjects fell into the Uninvolved category, meaning there was a lack of emotional involvement. At its extreme was a daughter who had not talked with her mother for several years. Nine of the eighty-eight respondents in my study also described themselves as uninvolved. At the extreme was Becky, a forty-one-year-old mother of one daughter. Becky's mother is an alcoholic who is also mentally ill. Becky says this about her mother:

> She told us all our lives that she never really wanted children, and when the grandchildren started coming she said they made her feel old, so she has rejected them also.

Becky keeps "tabs" on her mother through her sister, but doesn't have anything to do with her. Her mother has rejected her and the pain is evident in every line of Becky's questionnaire. She's working on the problems through counseling, but the dysfunctional patterns are also evident in Becky's relationship with her own daughter.

What's the Best Thing about Your Relationship with Your Mother?

Rosalind Barnett identified four aspects of our mother-daughter relationships that are most rewarding:

1. Having a mother who lets you know she cares about you
2. Having a mother who gets along well with the important people in your life—children, husband/partner, and friends
3. Having a close relationship with your mother
4. Getting along smoothly with your mother[6]

Being able to talk over problems with Mother, having her companionship, and knowing that she's always been there to help out when we need her adds a sense of comfort and security to our lives that is like money in our psychological and emotional banks.

My mom and I are very much alike and have always had a very strong kinship/friendship.

My mom is a caring individual who always encourages me to do my thing. She gave me "space" when I was growing up.

Suzanne writes this tribute to her mom:

I remember so plainly when I was about ten. You were to attend a special dinner with Dad out of town. You had a beautiful new dress and had looked forward to this event. I was suddenly taken ill with

blood poisoning and you stayed home. Dad went alone and you
attended to me. I never heard you complain.

A young mother of three writes about her mother who has just
turned fifty-two:

My mom grew up without a mom. Her five children who are now
adults all have special relationships with her. Her kids are successful, her marriage is successful, and her relationship with God is
successful.

The women who write such tributes to their mothers have amazing memory banks that will serve them well through their adult lives
and through all their relationships.

I know that my mother sounds almost too good to be true, but she was
really quite remarkable. She raised three children all by herself, gave
us many extra advantages—music lessons, art school, college—and
did it all with such grace and good cheer.

What Causes You the Most Concern about Your
Relationship with Your Mother?

Relationships with our mothers and daughters are like that proverbial
little girl with the curl in the middle of her forehead: when they are
good, they are very, very good, but when they are bad, they are
horrid.

Barnett identified the four items that caused women the most
concerns in relationships with their mothers:

❦

1. Seeing your mother age and worrying about how she will manage as she gets older
2. Feeling guilty or uncertain about your obligations to your mother
3. Having to act like a parent to your mother
4. A difficult or poor relationship with your mother[7]

We women deal with a wide range of negative emotions surrounding the aging of our mothers. Cohler and Grunebaum have found that

the need to rebalance dependency/independency often sets in motion a struggle between mother and daughter for control of the caregiving situation. Often, the psychological balance of power is held by the elderly parent.[8]

Many women in caretaker roles constantly struggle with their situation:

I've been caring for my mother for seven years and it's very confusing.

She is now totally dependent. She can no longer write, dress herself, or take responsibility for day-to-day activity. I've hired a daytime nurse when I'm at work. But she still wants to control my life.

We're coming to a point where she wants me to take care of her. I adore my mother, but I can't live with her. We are coming to a point of decision.

❦

Other women thoroughly enjoy the opportunity to spend time with their aging mothers.

> My mother's 95 and in a retirement home. I visit her often and always take coffee with me. We have always enjoyed drinking coffee together. When she is up to it, we go out for lunch or shopping together. My relationship with her now is healthier than it's ever been.

> Mother had a stroke four years before she died, and I had to help her a great deal and take her places. It was hard for her to give up her independence, but she was a person who never complained, and it was easy to do things for her. She would occasionally get discouraged, but she was really quite a remarkable woman, very sweet and very patient.

While a sizable number of women feel they are in Responsible Daughter/Dependent Mother roles with their own mothers, this aspect of their relationship does not seem to cause the stress and problems for them that the research literature would suggest. Of far more concern to them is the psychological/emotional hold their mothers still have over them, as evidenced by what they talk about when asked what they wish their mothers would stop doing. They want their mothers to stop giving unwanted advice and prying into their lives when they haven't been asked. They want their mothers to stop being so critical and unforgiving and to start loving them for who they are. They crave relationships with their mothers that are more satisfying.

> I'd like to say that I'd let her know me better, but I wouldn't trust her enough with the information.

❦

I wish that she had trusted me more.

I wish I'd gotten counseling for both of us.

I wish I could share more of my thoughts and feelings with her.

I wish I'd been more honest, in spite of her fear of confrontative discussions.

I wish I could talk more intimately with her.

Women also crave a close physical relationship with their mothers, particularly those whose mothers are deceased or live far away.

I wish I could be with her more often.

I wish I'd hugged and kissed her more and told her more often that I loved her.

I wish I'd been more physically responsive to her.

Our relationships with our mothers are filled with many regrets. In retrospect, we wish that petty issues hadn't kept us estranged.

I wish I'd respected her more as a youngster.

I wish I hadn't been so bratty and disrespectful to her in adolescence.

I wish I'd been more sensitive to her needs when she was an invalid during the last two and a half years of her life.

❦

I wish we could have been friends sooner and really enjoyed each other.

Although no mother-daughter relationship is perfect (nor could ever be), some of us are more filled with regret than others. We spend much of our time wishing things were—or had been—different.

In the next two chapters, we'll explore mother-daughter relationships that aren't working and offer some suggestions for improving and/or mending yours.

IT MAY BE

Maybe all that my verses have expressed
is simply what was never allowed to be:
only what was hidden and suppressed
from woman to woman, from family to
family.

The way that in my house tradition
was
the rule by which one did things
properly;
they say the women of my mother's
house
were always silent—yes, it well may
be.

Sometimes my mother felt longings to be free,
but then a bitter wave rose to her eyes
and in the shadows she wept.

And all this—caustic, betrayed,
chastised—all this that
in her soul she tightly kept,
I think that, without knowing, I have
set it free.
Alfonsina Storni *(translated from the Spanish*
by Mark Smith-Soto)

CHAPTER SEVEN

Mending the Broken Mother-Daughter Relationship
Understanding the Break

I didn't enjoy being around her. I felt like I couldn't do anything right and she didn't understand me or my life.

I wish she could change. I'd like a relationship with her like I have with my daughters, unconditional love and the opportunity for her to really know me and me to know her.
MOTHER OF THREE

As I REREAD THE QUESTIONNAIRES OF THE EIGHTY-EIGHT women who participated in this study, I can do so with objectivity in eighty-seven cases. I am not connected to them in any way. There is one, however, that I return to over and over. I not only carefully read the lines in a handwriting that is very similar to mine, but I read between the lines and look for hidden meanings. It is the questionnaire of my sister. Ten years my junior, she remains a virtual stranger to me. I left home when she was eight years old, and the circumstances of our lives and the choices I made only further served to estrange us. After reading her questionnaire, I wanted to talk with her in person. The things she said helped me understand more about why I felt the way I did about my mother and why I had made the choices I did.

My sister and I will meet later this month; she is entertaining me in her home in another state. I will get to know her husband and three children. Perhaps we will like each other, perhaps not. But one thing is certain, we will now begin collectively to make sense of our lives as women. We will now begin to explore how the woman who was our mother has really shaped our lives. The last time we met was at our mother's funeral in 1985. My sister was angry. I had not been at my mother's bedside during her last months as she died of liver cancer. I know I was in part to blame for her unhappy later years. If I had been there for her, perhaps things would have been different. I had called in those last months to tell her that I loved her many times, but I did not go to her. In my heart, I'm hoping that reconciliation with my sister will please my mother in heaven and that I, in turn, will begin to understand and have the compassion for my mother that I could never show while she was alive.

As you will see in this chapter, each story of mother-daughter estrangement is unique. But I hope that you will also see that "the process of healing includes seeing one's mother as other than oneself, recognizing that she is the legatee of her mother's behavior, and acknowledging how terribly limited her choices may have been."[1]

I have only just begun to look at my mother's life from her perspective instead of mine. She grew up as the only girl in a family of boys, indulged by a loving father but always made uneasy and

❦

unsure by an undemonstrative and hyper-critical mother. That lack of self-confidence was only exacerbated when her new husband moved her to the country to live in isolation in a small apartment above his parents' farm home. There my mother would encounter the first of many rivalries to my father's divided love: his sister. A self-assured, fun-loving, and beautiful woman, my aunt lived with her parents and was the apple of not only their eyes but her five brothers as well, particularly my father. My shy, quiet mother had a difficult time assimilating into this family of rowdy boys and their beautiful sister. She was proper and contained. They were boisterous and outspoken. Her restraint was interpreted as condescension, her quiet nature as laziness and lack of involvement. She was in many ways doomed from the start.

She focused on becoming a good mother, but her first-born (Elaine) was a challenging child whose personality was similar to her husband's family: boisterous, quick-moving, and energetic. She had a difficult time coping with two such high-energy individuals. She often sent her daughter downstairs to spend time with her aunt and paternal grandmother or to spend weekends with her own mother and older brother who had never married and still lived at home. She took afternoon naps to regain the strength lost from several debilitating pregnancies and miscarriages. She was expected to be strong and uncomplaining through it all. Her husband worked long hours since he was in business for himself.

The second rivalry for my father's love was his work. He immersed himself in it and was excited about it. She had bouts of depression. She had many allergies and bordered on asthmatic and was ill a great deal. Her husband indulged her but rarely took her seriously.

With a growing family of three children, a boy and another girl, she became the quintessential Christian mother. She taught Sunday school, was active in the women's missionary group, and entertained almost weekly. Her husband's sister now lived next door, and my mother was frequently reminded of my aunt's ability to work, keep her house, and still have time to entertain her brothers almost every night around her kitchen table. My mother never shared those good times around the kitchen table. She went to bed before her husband came home from work. He didn't understand why.

She reveled in the accomplishments of her older daughter, an honor student and musician. Her daughter could always be found playing the piano or organ at every church service, and she would fairly bust her buttons at this pleasurable experience. She often said that even the most disagreeable task was easier if she could listen to her daughter play. But this daughter also became a rival for her husband's love. Her oldest daughter and her husband were soulmates. Their interest in the world of work, their energy and outgoing personalities made her feel left out on many occasions.

The person she was most connected to was her own mother, a bright but often mean-spirited and critical woman. They talked each day on the telephone, and whatever happened in the household had to pass Grandma's muster first of all. There were dozens of rules that governed our lives, but they basically all boiled down to "What will Grandma Larson say?" Her husband looked upon this with amusement and mild annoyance. He didn't realize that his wife had never separated from her mother.

She was a good mother. She always cooked marvelous meals and had her children's clothes cleaned and pressed. She had standards to uphold. She led her children to believe they were somehow different and better than those with whom they went to school in the "country." There was an order and structure to life that seldom varied: washing on Monday, ironing on Tuesday, cleaning the bedrooms on Wednesday, cleaning the rest of the house on Thursday,

❧

shopping on Friday, and getting ready for Sunday on Saturday. The world was measured in terms of how much she accomplished around the house, and cleanliness was next to godliness. She and her oldest daughter would frequently argue about the necessity of keeping a clean room, and usually she would win all arguments. Church and Bible reading were a regular part of family life, and she reminded her husband often of the importance of rules. He broke them on occasion, and his children always knew that he was the only one who could get away with it. Grandma couldn't touch him. She was always slightly in awe, though somewhat disapproving of him.

When her first husband died, she found a man who could rescue her from having to be independent and make her own decisions. He took away the last vestige of her self-worth by doing the shopping, the cleaning, and cooking. She was to be the princess. He would take care of her. He was a controlling and self-serving man. She was hospitalized once for depression, but the real problems were very deep-seated. She was never able to overcome her obsession with her own condition and summon the strength to celebrate any part of her life.

If I as her daughter had been able to judge my mother in the context of her life, I might have been able to accept and love her for what she was, a needy and vulnerable woman who just wanted me to be with her but could never verbalize her desires. Instead, I wanted the perfection from my mother that I'd been led to believe was my due. I wanted my mother to be the model mother and grandmother to my children, and when she couldn't fulfill that role, I cut her out of my life. I left her household feeling that I could do anything, but the one thing I was never able to do while she was living was to forgive my mother for being human.

❦

What Keeps Mothers and Daughters from Being Friends?

Of the eighty-eight women who completed my questionnaire, sixteen (18%) have what can best be described as "unfinished business" with their own mothers. They fall into five categories:

1. They have chosen to be uninvolved with their mothers (as I did).
2. They are engaged in major conflicts with their mothers characterized by frequent confrontations.
3. They carry blame and accusation in their hearts for what their mothers have done to them, which frequently results in feelings of low self-esteem.
4. They are enmeshed in relationships with their own daughters that replicate the dysfunctional relationships they have (had) with their own mothers.
5. Their mothers are deceased and their deaths did not put to rest unresolved issues in their relationships.

In many cases, the respondents are enduring conflictual relationships, low self-esteem, and poor relationships with both their mothers and daughters simultaneously. Their lives are hanging from a slender thread.

Understanding Maternal Behavior

It is not possible to mend a broken mother-daughter relationship until we gain a clear understanding of the fives types of maternal behavior that can have a devastating impact on a daughter's self-esteem and ability to function as a whole person. The labels are the work of Victoria Secunda, who has developed the composites.[2]

❦

You need to remember, however, that the composites define the extremes, and while each of us may be and probably is guilty of isolated occasions of such behaviors, the woman who exhibits these behaviors as a constant norm is the only one for whom the label can be genuinely applied. The stories belong to the women I surveyed.

The Doormat

My own mother was a perfect example of a doormat.

> The Doormat is a woman of heartbreaking weakness and dependency who valiantly tries to do what her husband and children ask of her, if only she could muster the energy and will. There is not a trace of rancor in her—indeed, she gives the impression that she is a victim of life's inequities, a prey for the meanspirited, taking the blame for everyone.[3]

As my father lay dying, he pulled his sister close to him. "Take care of Vi," he whispered. "She'll never be able to take care of herself." My aunt was to become my mother's new husband.

Doormats are, as Victoria Secunda wrote, "unable to defend themselves, obliterating their own needs and instead punishing themselves. They believe that anything that goes wrong in their lives or families is their fault—they sit as their own judge and jury, unable to mount any defense, and accept unquestioningly their own verdict of unworthiness." It was this sense of unworthiness on my mother's part that I found so frightening. I felt that her neediness would somehow suck me in and diminish my own sense of well-being and worth. I was afraid that she would ruin my marriage if my husband suspected he might have to "parent" my mother.

I'd always known that my mother was kind, good, generous, and loving. It didn't make sense that I could feel so angry toward her

❦

when she'd been such a nice person. I couldn't really explain it to myself, and I certainly couldn't explain it to anyone else. Now I know I was afraid I might become like her.

Meg's mother is also a doormat. Meg is the forty-six-year-old mother of a high-school student. She has earned two master's degrees and works full-time at a responsible research and teaching position. Meg can't take large doses of her mother and so from time to time withdraws for "recuperation." She stops writing and phoning, growing increasingly irritated and impatient over her mother's lack of responsibility for her own life and her constant blaming of everyone else for her unhappiness. As Meg completed the questionnaire, she had her own "aha," which happened to many of the women as they searched their souls for the answers to my questions. She writes:

> The interesting thread I see in all of this is my wish to be more accepting and tolerant of the two major women in my life.

Meg realized as she wrote how critical she had been of her daughter's low-key and relaxed approach to life.

> Perhaps I should look to my daughter more in this regard as I believe she possesses those qualities of tolerance and patience that I do not.

The Critic

Five of the women in my study appear to have genuine Critics for mothers. Oh, all of our mothers point out how we might improve from time to time, and we do the same for our daughters. That's the nature of having a relationship with another human being. But the real Critics have the sword of the put-down honed to a razor-sharp edge. As one daughter said:

❧

I wish my mother would stop looking for flaws in me. We've never been estranged openly. We've made a pretense of a normal relationship, but her criticisms hold me at arm's length. I asked her for forgiveness once for my resentfulness and she replied: "It's about time."

Vonda's mother is such an individual. Most mothers would have been beaming with pride to watch their middle-aged daughter walk across the platform to receive her master's degree. Vonda's mother wondered when she'd get her doctorate. Typical of many Critic mothers, Vonda's mom loves to give her the silent treatment. Fighting would be beneath her.

Her silent treatment destroys me. She won't argue so we can come out feeling close.

Vonda was tormented by her mother's silences as a child and felt guilty and manipulated all at the same time. Although they live in the same town and see each other from time to time, Vonda feels that she and her mother have no real emotional involvement. But she continues to try to break through the barrier of criticism and negativism that have characterized this mother-daughter relationship. She desperately wants to connect. Vonda recently gave her mother a tub railing because she'd fallen in the shower, and her mother reacted with anger and criticism. Vonda confronted her mother about it in a quiet way and feels that her patience and willingness to be assertive paid off when she later received a thank-you note.

Vonda is a woman of deep faith with two bright and vibrant daughters, one in high school and the other in college. Her own intelligence and understanding of her mother's problem is making her doubly aware of her relationships with her daughters. Her own personal prayer life, the development of good communication skills, and the support and encouragement of a loving spouse are her keys to success with her daughters.

Patti has reconciled with her Critic mother through the help of books, friends, and counseling. Her daughter's eating disorder forced the family into therapy and brought Patti face-to-face with the estrangement she had unconsciously created in order to survive. She feels her reconciliation is complete, and she is able to say that "I know my mother, I accept my mother, and I love my mother." Her brother was not as fortunate as Patti. He was not able to break the dependency bonds and committed suicide. Patti is energized by her newfound independence and is attending graduate school in a new field of study.

The Smotherer

Mothers who smother fool the rest of us. They look like the mothers everyone would want. Kelly, an exuberant and vivacious stay-at-home mom whose mother sounds like a Smotherer, said just that: "Many friends wished that my mother was their mother." But a wistful tone crept into her response when asked what she liked least about her mother:

> I'm forty-two years old and she *still* gives me advice on everything. This sounds terrible, but she's also hard to talk to when you are complaining about someone because she always takes up for the other person. My mother likes to control me in many ways. I wish she'd stop giving me advice when I don't ask for it. But she bails me out of many over-spending jams. She's always there with the cash!

These behaviors are typical of a Smotherer. It isn't just that Smotherers identify with their daughters—all mothers do that, to a degree.

Rather, it is that their maternity is a mandate to coerce their daughters into the mother's image of what a "happy childhood" is all about, and to that end will sacrifice themselves with unsullied moral certainty and tireless stamina. The Smotherer wants to boost the odds that her daughter will be carefree and popular, the happiest little girl in the world.[4]

Kelly's mother is a gourmet cook and made sure that Kelly ate plenty. Her mom is thin, but Kelly's weight problem plagues her. Kelly's mom "was like Beaver Cleaver's mom. She was always dressed nicely and in control." Kelly has turned into the carefree little girl her mother set out to create. "My mom is wild and crazy," her son says. "She wants to be a teenager when she grows up."

The Avenger

When you meet the daughter of an Avenger, anything your mother has ever done or will do pales in comparison. The Avenger mother is

addicted to creating discord; one fight blends into another in a long crescendo and diminuendo of domestic disharmony. Her first victim is her spouse who, for psychological reasons of his own, seems to be equally addicted to the friction between them. Frequently his marriage is a repetition of his relationship to another Avenger—his mother or father.[5]

Kate's mother and father were alcoholics. They had many verbal and physical fights and finally divorced when she was fourteen. With poignancy Kate shares the experiences of her adolescent years:

> The kids had to go to work and give our money to our mother. We wore hand-me-downs and got help from church. Mom blew all of our money and said we owed it to her because she was our mom. She went out to eat a lot, but when she stayed home she would sometimes sit at the table and eat a steak while we only had oatmeal. She said we didn't deserve good food, but she did because if she wasn't strapped with seven kids she could have anything she wanted.

As Victoria Secunda stated,

> The Avenger works carefully to destroy her child's sense of self. Unless the daughter can summon some miraculous inner strength, or find elsewhere the supportive affection that will help her to feel good about herself—which some daughters manage to do—she will not have the will to extricate herself from her mother's tyranny.[6]

Kate is still working desperately on this process. She could not "connect" with her own children (a daughter and four sons) for years because she had no example from her childhood. She is reliving the pain of her own adolescence as she watches her seventeen-year-old daughter's self-destructive behavior. Her daughter has run away from home and refuses to come back. Kate became depressed and suicidal. She hasn't given up on either her mother or her daughter, however. There is a quiet desperation in her heart as she writes tributes to both of them on the questionnaire: "I would like to thank my mother for giving me life. It is the finest

❦

gift she has ever given." And to her daughter: "Despite all of the difficulties in our relationship, I love my daughter very much. I know with time and help, she can become at peace with herself and others. She has great potential to be a very giving and loving person."

The Deserter

Mothers who desert their daughters fall into four categories according to Secunda: the psychotic mother, the alcoholic or drug-addicted mother, the non-attached mother, and the deceased Bad Mommy.[7]

Gail's mother was a Deserter. She deserted her physically on many occasions. Her mother once left her in a day-care center overnight when she was four years old. The memory is a painful one for Gail. She began caring for herself and making all her own decisions when she was eight years old; she thought everyone did. She was always sent away to summer camps. But the physical abandonment was secondary to her mother's emotional and psychological abandonment. Her mother's psychotic state made her psychologically unavailable. Even though her family had plenty of money, Gail didn't have the reassurance, the tenderness, and the comfort of a loving mother's arms.

Now Gail visits her mother once a year in the nursing home where her mother lives in a far Western state. Her mother has been placed on a behavior management plan and is separated from her husband, to whom she was abusive. Several professionals have diagnosed her personality as psychotic.

Gail has only recently come to realize the depth of her abandonment. She is still amazingly philosophical about her mother, but the counseling she's been through during her divorce and problems with her own daughter is just beginning to uncover what her therapist believes is deep psychological and emotional abuse. "I thought I had a pretty happy childhood," she says wistfully. Her own personal hell is her thirty-year-old daughter's abandonment of her, the silent treatment she sometimes receives from her second husband, and the constant battles with her first husband over college tuition for their youngest son.

Several women lost their mothers to death at critical periods in their development. The "desertion" of their mothers is of a different kind. Children of mothers who die prematurely eventually emerge from their terrible loss with the capacity for love and hope if their relationships with their mothers, while alive, were loving and supportive and steady. But if the relationship was ambivalent or unhappy, the child is wedged between grief and anger.

Carmen was only twelve hours old when her mother died and only recently has come to realize that the stepmother whom her father married when she was a year-and-a-half old really does love her. When she was growing up she always felt like a stepchild. She still is emotional about her experiences:

> I honestly felt she loved my brothers more because they were hers. She wasn't very flexible or supportive of my personality. I'm very close to my mother's sister. We are very similar—creative, high energy, overly involved, leaders and doers.

Margaret also lost her mother when she was very young. Her maternal grandmother stepped in to fill the mother role, which created a different set of problems for Margaret. Her father moved in with his parents after Margaret's mother died when she was two, and her strong-willed and very religious grandmother became her mother. Margaret was a warm and responsive child who hugged her grandmother a lot, but her grandmother wasn't free with her return of affection. A victim of Alzheimers, Margaret's grandmother now

❧

lives in a nursing home, and Margaret is coping with conflicting emotions—grief for the mother she never knew, anger at her grandmother for refusing to accept her as an adult, and guilt because she hasn't been able to fully meet the needs of someone who sacrificed for her. There is a pervasive sadness in Margaret's responses, a deep regret for what could have been.

Understanding Our Responses, as Daughters

Our responses as daughters to these extremes in mothering are just as extreme. Secunda believes that our behavior will fall into one or two of the following five categories: The Angel, The Superachiever, The Cipher, The Troublemaker, and The Defector.[8] Once again a caveat is in order for the reader since the composites define the extremes. While each of us may and probably can be described by one of these labels, the woman who exhibits these behaviors as a constant norm is the only one for whom the label can be genuinely applied.

The Angel
The Angel is described by Secunda in this way:

> Angels are the standard-bearers of the family's younger generation and are burdened with enormous responsibilities: Do well in school, don't get into trouble, set an example for your brothers and sisters. And the biggest responsibilities are these: Be there when Mommy needs you and Don't bring Mommy any bad news.[9]

Often the oldest girl or first born in her family, the Angel becomes the "mommy" in the family to her younger brothers and sisters.

My friend Rhonda fulfilled such a role in her family. The oldest of nine children, she became the family nanny. Her mother relied on her to

❧

feed, bathe, and nurture the younger siblings. All of her siblings have married and are raising families of their own. Rhonda is still single and sorting out through therapy why she has never married.

The Superachiever

The Superachiever identifies with the men in her world. It isn't that the Superachiever wants to be a man, but that she "wants to be as good as men in the work world, because there it is usually men, rather than women, who have the power to make things happen and to be in control. The Superachiever would rather die than be vulnerable or dependent."[10] Superachievers have a difficult time mothering daughters. They cannot let their daughters fail or lose, and they become controlling and impatient in their quest to create perfection in their daughters.

Chris, a successful professional woman, is the superachieving daughter of a critical and unhappy mother. She writes of her own daughter, Susie:

> The biggest point of conflict between us is her lack of assertiveness. I want to push her to strive for goals she doesn't care about reaching.

Interestingly enough, as Chris completed the questionnaire, she experienced a moment of insight into the traps she had fallen into with both her mother and her teenage daughter.

Corrine, another high-powered superachiever who practices law in a downtown firm, bemoans her daughter Amy's lack of motivation, saying that she doesn't even *try*.

The Cipher

The Cipher, as the label implies, has internalized a sense of invisibility and lack of self-worth. Ciphers are the daughters of avenging or critical mothers who were never able to rise above the barrage of expectations and criticisms that battered their existence. They are always worried about offending someone and even though they may marry remain tied to their mothers through adulthood.

Connie is a Cipher. At the age of 47 after twenty-three years of marriage she wonders if she should have married at all.

> I have not been always sure that I really should have married. There is so much involved in being a good wife that doesn't appeal to me. Perhaps I'm too selfish.

Her eighty-eight-year-old mother, though feeble and frail, holds a viselike grip on Connie's sense of well-being and worth.

> I have always felt unable to feel or act like a mature adult in her presence. Also I somehow always feel defensive when I'm around her. This is a problem probably because she has lived with us ever since the third year of our marriage. I don't know if the fault is hers or mine.

The Troublemaker

The Troublemaker is the black sheep of the family. She stands ready to take the blame for whatever happens in her family. She is rebellious and outspoken, filled with a seething rage that often masks a deep sense of self-doubt. As a mother herself, the Troublemaker has the best of intentions. She starts out well, but as soon as her daughter develops a will and mind of her own, the Troublemaker begins to reenact her own explosive relationship with her mother, and the power struggles ensue.

Charlotte might be described as a Troublemaker:

> Compromise and keeping the peace are more important to my mother than equality. Equality is important to me. She manipulates. I hit it head on.

❧

Charlotte is never afraid to take on the world. At the age of 44 she's taken on three husbands since college and during the last six years has held five different upper-level management positions. In her words:

> I've always believed women were entitled and able to do whatever they chose. The women's movement had little impact on my choices. I was never much for "organized movements." I always had my own!

Charlotte is currently contemplating a fourth marriage but is mellowing in her middle years, thinking more about how she does things and what she wants to do with her remaining time on earth. She feels she's more patient now, although she still has a pretty complex life. She is a self-proclaimed "change agent," and as she hopscotches from job to job she stirs up the status quo, always evoking strong responses, both positive and negative, from all she meets. She and her only daughter, Mary, were separated recently when she took a new job across the country. Mary chose to remain with friends to finish her senior year in high school. Charlotte feels her daughter doesn't have the self-control or the maturity to handle the situation, but she states: "Mary, as per usual, claimed she did!"

The Defector

The final category of daughters is The Defector. Defectors are characterized by the following:

> They had virtually no relationship with their fathers, who were either as cruel as their mothers or failed to intervene on their daughters' behalf; they were victims of either child abuse or incest; they had parents who were alcoholics; and they felt like outsiders within the family.[11]

❧

Vange is a Defector. Through her acceptance of Christ and active counseling, the hostility, anger, and self-loathing that characterized her life are beginning to fade. Vange's father was sexually abusive to her, and both parents ridiculed her, making her feel inferior, unloved, and unimportant. They divorced when she was fourteen, and Vange became a parent to her seven younger siblings. She is now in her third marriage, a stable and loving relationship. But unfortunately the vicious cycle of her own childhood was repeated in her daughter's life before Vange recognized her need for help. Cynthia, who is now seventeen, has also defected, and Vange has been estranged and separated from her mother for years.

Excess Baggage

As you have already begun to see, we bring to our mother-daughter relationships excess baggage from a variety of places. Not only do we bring our own personal experiences, but in addition we must overcome the conventional wisdom and "myths" that pervade society's thinking about mother-daughter relationships. In her wonderful book, *Don't Blame Mother: Mending the Mother-Daughter Relationship*, Paula Caplan lists nine myths that perpetuate mother-blaming and keep us from fully experiencing a satisfying mother-daughter relationship. She calls four of them the "Perfect Mother Myths" and the remaining five the "Bad Mother Myths."[12]

Perfect Mother Myths
Myth One would have us believe that "the measure of a good mother is a perfect daughter." We are bound to follow the rules that our mothers set forth for us. Even at the age of fifty I sometimes (not always) apologize to someone for not having cleaned my house. "Who cares about whether or not the house is cleaned?" they query me. "I came to

❧

see you, not your house." It's my mother looking over my shoulder. She cleaned the living room on Thursdays, therefore so should I. If we're not perfect then somehow it must be our mothers' faults.

Myth Two would have us believe that "mothers are endless founts of nurturance." Mary Pride contributes to this myth in her book *The Way Home: Beyond Feminism, Back to Reality*, when she states:

> God intended women to spend their whole lives serving other people. Young women serve their children, their mothers, their husbands, and the community at large. Older women train and assist the younger women, and in some cases become church helpers. Women are not called to pursue motherhood for five years, get a career, and thereafter live for themselves. We are responsible for keeping society healthy and human.[13]

Mary says nothing about who will meet our needs when our children go off to make lives of their own or our husbands die and leave us with mortgages. Perhaps she has not lived long enough for those things to happen to her.

This myth of motherhood that says we must endlessly nurture with never a thought of our own needs results in some of the mother-blaming that most of us indulge in. We expect everything from our mothers. And when we only get a portion of what we expect, we blame. We forgive our fathers if they're not there. After all, they're supposed to be at work earning a living for us. They aren't expected to listen endlessly to our petty problems. We'll allow our fathers to be human. But:

> because of the double standard, we often focus on what our mothers have failed to do, without considering why they might have failed. Sometimes mothers fail to meet their daughters'

❧

needs because other family members need them, too. Or a mother may be a single mother, an immigrant mother or a mother of color coping with the consequences of racism; she may be a disabled mother, a mother on welfare, a mother who is physically ill or depressed or anxious, a mother juggling paid work and housework, a mother with a depressed, alcoholic, or abusive partner, or a mother with many children or with a young, ill, or disabled child. And all mothers sometimes fail simply because we are human.[14]

Perfect Mother Myth Three would have us believe that mothers naturally know how to raise children. Since we're women ourselves, raising daughters ought to be really easy. But as most of us have experienced:

Women do not have a handy gland called "mother" which is mysteriously activated upon giving birth. Contrary to every myth perpetrated on us throughout history, not all women make good mothers, just as all men don't make good plumbers. That we can give birth does not guarantee that we can also mother success-fully.[15]

The final myth that makes it difficult for mothers and daughters to get past the blaming stage is that "good mothers and good daughters don't get angry." Getting angry is considered by most to be unaccep-table female behavior. Consequently even a little anger can make both mothers and daughters suppress this emotion and back off from confrontation, which then leads to further estrangement, either physical or emotional. A well-known Christian author has felt the underlying tension for forty years but has made a pretense of a normal relationship: "My mother held me at arms' length." Another woman, a career counselor, avoids conflict at all costs: "I accept my mother the way she is and base our relationship on her terms."

Bad Mother Myths

"Bad Mother Myths"[16] can turn perfectly ordinary mothers into a caricature of Cinderella's evil stepmother. The first Bad Mother Myth is that mothers are inferior to fathers. That was the norm in our family, and I blush to think of how I participated in this travesty around my kitchen table. I wouldn't tolerate it for a minute in my own house or office, but my mother was consistently the butt of amusing jokes and a not-so-subtle insinuation that we were all better than she was. No wonder she suffered from low self-esteem. Her husband and her children did nothing to build her up. Men did the most important work in the world. That's why I wanted to go off with my father to work and frequently did, even as young as six or seven. Kim Chernin summarizes my own feelings in *Reinventing Eve* when she writes:

> When the daughter at the crossroads rejects her mother and chooses her father instead, it is because she cannot find within the mother-world a way to grow into the full promise of her original female being.[17]

The second Bad Mother Myth would have us believe that "only the experts know how to raise children." And guess who most of the experts are? With regard to my own writing in the field of Christian parenting I frequently encounter the "male" experts who write authoritatively on childrearing. Almost without exception these experts have no firsthand knowledge of what it really means to parent children. They aren't doing it themselves. Their wives are. And even for their wives, raising children is terribly complex. We can't always

❦

figure out why anything happens in the way it does. But the "experts" are out there telling us that we ought to be able to do it perfectly.

The third Bad Mother Myth is that "mothers (and daughters) are bottomless pits of neediness." This neediness scares off both mothers and daughters. We worry that we will become trapped in this pit and be unable to live our own lives. We forget that "when someone close to us is upset, the best thing to do is simply to be present and listen, or wait empathetically and lovingly. We feel helpless and useless if we believe we should be able to banish their pain." I wish that I had thought more insightfully about this particular myth when my mother was going through her own personal hell of depression.

Myth Four would have us believe that mother-daughter closeness is unhealthy. As mothers we constantly worry about whether we've nurtured independence in our children. At the Wellesley College Center for Research on Women, researchers are finding that the emphasis for women on separating from their mothers has resulted in women being affirmed for this emotional distance, when in reality what is needed is what psychologist Janet Surrey calls "relational ability." Surrey and her group at Wellesley have found that "women do not want to separate from their mothers. They want to keep that relationship authentic and add other strong and close relationships.[18]

If we want to have healthy relationships as mothers and daughters, we need to throw out all our preconceived notions of what a mother or a daughter should be, all the "bad" or "good" myths that are floating around. But with all that said and done, where do we go from there? How can we mend broken mother-daughter relationships? How can we improve the bond we already have as women?

The next chapter will help you do exactly that.

❦

For more information ...

Bassoff, Evelyn Silten. *Mothering Ourselves: Help and Healing for Adult Daughters*. New York: Dutton, 1990.

Secunda, Victoria. *When You and Your Mother Can't Be Friends: Resolving the Most Complicated Relationship of Your Life*. New York: Delacorte Press, 1990.

CHAPTER EIGHT

Improving Your Mother-Daughter Relationships

Nobody's family can hang out the sign,
"nothing the matter here."
CHINESE PROVERB

IF YOU RECOGNIZE YOURSELF IN ANY OF THE DESCRIPTIONS OF mothers and daughters in Chapter Seven and want to improve your own relationship with either your mother or your daughter, there are a variety of positive ways to begin. Various psychotherapists offer many suggestions and solutions. I've put together the best of the suggestions in this section. For more in-depth information, consult the list of resources at the end of this chapter.

Three Essential Steps toward Mending a Relationship

Paula Caplan, who has written widely on the mother-daughter relationship, offers some very positive suggestions in her most recent book, *Don't Blame Mother*. She feels there are three essential steps to follow:

1. *Humanize your image of your mother,* because whether you discuss your problems with her or you just try to think in new ways about them, you need to see the real woman behind the mother-myths.
2. *Forge an alliance with your mother,* either in fact or in your own mind.
3. *Choose and define a problem on which to begin.*[1]

Humanizing your image

I personally took Caplan's first suggestion by writing my mother's biography, which appeared at the beginning of Chapter Seven. I talked with other people about what they remembered of her life and was surprised to find out that my cousin, who lived next door, had idolized her. In fact, she often wished that my mother were hers. Ironically, I often had the same wish about *her* mother. Columnist Anna Quindlen comments on this strange inability we have to see our mothers as others see them.

> My friends speak about their mothers, about their manipulations and criticisms and pointed remarks, and when I meet these same women I can recognize very little of them in the child's description. They usually seem intelligent, thoughtful, kind. But I am not in a position to judge. To me they are simply people, not some lifelong foil, a yardstick by which to measure

❦

myself, to publicly find Mother wanting, to privately find the fault within.

Writing my mother's biography helped me to see how bound she was by her own mother's critical spirit, a husband who was largely insensitive to her artistic spirit, and the physical demands of constant pregnancies. Were she still alive, I would hope that we could talk about her experiences and that I could ask her forgiveness face-to-face for my lack of empathy for her personal dilemmas. One woman developed a new appreciation and understanding of her mother when she read the over fifty love letters her father had written during World War II. She says, "It was very enlightening to see her through his eyes."

Forging an alliance

Forging an alliance between you and your mother begins by specifically asking your mother about her view of the relationship between the two of you. Caplan suggests pretending that you are a stranger who has just met your mother at a party and is listening to her describe her daughter and herself.[2]

Choosing and defining a problem

The third step suggested by Caplan is choosing and defining a specific problem on which to work. After identifying the problem (and it must be a problem that can be isolated and defined), the next step is to identify the feelings that you and your mother (or daughter) have about the problem. Many women have begun to work through these steps on their own. A nursing supervisor, Liz, is the mother of two daughters. She comments:

My mother's original definition of love was obedience. She was an obedient daughter whose mother never said "I love you." My disobedience made my mother realize she had been a good daughter and that gave her the strength to accept my love without total obedience.

After some rocky years, Liz, age 44, and her mother, age 72, have an excellent relationship. Liz read widely and consulted a counselor. She needed to make her own choices. Reconciliation was gradual, but patience and love brought her mother around.

As the women completed the questionnaires, they began to recognize that their mothers' lives had not been easy. Coral says,

> My mother has lived through many hardships. I respect her flexibility and courage in life. She was the seventh of eight children and very poor. She received the most education of all of her family. It didn't go to her head. I do love her and am feeling it right now. I have hope for more change.

Marie wishes she had shared more of her hurts and grief with her mother earlier in life. She wishes her mom would realize that "just because I have negative thoughts doesn't mean she's a bad mother. She tends to equate the two."

Seeing our mothers as human beings, taking the time to listen to what our mothers think and feel about our relationship, and beginning to work on one specific problem are three important beginning steps in improving mother-daughter relationships.

Three Relationship Options

As daughters and/or mothers, we have three relationship options open to us—friendship, truce, or divorce.

❦

Friendship

True mother-daughter friendships are possible only after many hurdles have been cleared. Both parties have to be willing to forgive and forget the mother's parenting mistakes and the daughter's rebellion. All of the Good and Bad Mother Myths that were mentioned in Chapter Seven must be transcended. And, most of all, a new definition of the mother-daughter relationship must be written. An important component of friendship is the ability to overlook some of the worst aspects of a person's character or personality because we cherish the positive aspects even more. "But we don't want our mothers to have any bad stuff, yet we want them to love us in spite of our bad stuff, just as they want us to love them."[3]

Kay Marshall Strom, in her book, *Making Friends with Your Mother,* suggests some bylaws for daughters attempting to build friendships with mothers.[4] They read like a laundry list of bylaws for building successful relationships with anyone—spouses, friends, and children. They include communicating effectively, sharing perspectives, accepting differences, spending time, taking the initiative, being patient and affirming, and respecting individuality and privacy. Often it's much easier to be forgiving, patient, and accepting of perfect strangers. We don't expect them to be perfect. But our moms?

Truce

If you can't develop a true peerlike friendship with your mother, the next best thing is a truce. Many women fall into this category. They have decided that true friendship is an unobtainable goal, but they don't want to totally divorce themselves from their mothers, either. They are maintaining a middle ground that, while it is not generally characterized by conflict or strife, does not resemble the ideal of peerlike friendship either. To achieve a state of truce when the relationship has been characterized by strife and conflict requires that time limits be set, particularly in the case of critical and avenging mothers. These time limits are similar to the "time-outs" some parents use in disciplining their children. If your mother launches into a vindictive diatribe, take a time-out, explaining that you'll come back when she's through.

Some women need to take brief time-outs from their relationships with their mothers. Anne Marie needs "to withdraw and recuperate" before resuming calls and letters to her Critic mother. Others attempt to maintain an emotional neutrality that avoids discussion of deep issues. Corrine put it this way when asked about her relationship with her mother:

> I could write a book. My relationship with my mom is not the relationship of my dreams, but I have come to terms with what it can be and accept it as the best we can do for one another.

The second prerequisite for a truce relationship is the ability to control one's reactions. We must understand how our mother's guilt, weakness, or criticism can trigger unhealthy reactions in us personally and then begin to disarm these reactions.

Divorce

Just as divorce in a marriage relationship leaves scars on all the participants, divorce of mothers and daughters brings with it pain. The divorcing daughter will be the object of criticism from family and pity from friends. Before you do make the decision to separate from your mother, be sure you have no other alternatives. And sometimes there are none. When mothers are systematically and deliberately destroying their daughters, there are no other choices. But in the words of Victoria Secunda,

> If you find you must let go, know that your mother is more to be pitied, and it isn't your fault that she can't be loving to you on any level. Your lovability is not contingent on whether or not she loves you. Mourn your loss and you will be able to develop your own talent for loving, for being friends with your children when they are grown, and for creating out of your desperate history a whole and optimistic future.[5]

There's a price to pay for divorce, however. There are tears of regret for unresolved problems and pangs of guilt for what remained unspoken. And when mothers die, as mine did, the unresolved problems can never be addressed.

Forgiveness

For the best in mother-daughter relationships what is needed is the healing balm of forgiveness.

> To forgive is to give up a resentment against someone and to need neither material nor emotional reward for the grievance. The act of forgiveness requires that we take control of our life, that we not be its victim. Forgiveness leads to self-renewal. It is, at the same time, a humbling and empowering experience. We surrender ourselves to what is and was without the fight that demands our life be different and we empower ourselves by letting go of the past, the excuses, the blame. We stand fully human, in its best sense, when we can forgive.[6]

Forgiveness is not easy. It requires listening, touching, and loving. It requires incredible humility. But women are learning how to forgive. They are rebuilding relationships with their mothers and daughters through forgiveness and with the help of professional counselors and God's healing love.

Helpful Guidelines for Mothers and Daughters

Julie and Dorothy Firman have developed a set of helpful guidelines for mothers and daughters based on their workshops with hundreds of mothers and daughters.[7]

For moms
First, here's some advice for us as mothers.

Don't give advice. A mother's advice creates feelings of deficiency and inadequacy (as evidenced by the women in the survey). As difficult as it may be, you need to hold your tongue.

Don't rescue. Let your daughter solve her own problems and stand on her own two feet. Good friends give support and encouragement; they don't fix things.

Don't interfere. Even though you as a mother are more mature and have "all the answers," step back and allow your daughter to make her own mistakes.

Don't send your daughter on a guilt trip. There's nothing more devastating to a relationship than manipulating, plotting, or coercing your daughter to do something by using guilt as the motivator.

Don't remember the "good old days." Each of us has to live our own lives. Reminding your daughter of what you went through intimates that you don't recognize that she is an individual living in a different time and place.

❧

Don't fake it. Don't subjugate your own needs in order to placate your daughter. If you have problems together, confront them together. Pretending won't make them go away.

For daughters

And now we put on our other hat—that of a daughter. Here is the Firmans' advice for us as daughters.

Take her off her pedestal. React to your mother as you would a good friend or a stranger. Give her the same benefit of the doubt.

Don't interpret. It's very dangerous to constantly read old feelings and ideas into new situations. When in doubt, do some double-checking. Look for the positives rather than the negatives.

Don't carry expectations. You can't be both an adult and a child. Treat your mother like another adult—not like she's the adult, and you're the child.

Create boundaries. Let your mother know who you are and what you want in clear, concise, and kind terms.

Don't send your mother on a guilt trip. An honest direct approach is much more effective than playing for sympathy.

I hope that reading *My Mother, My Daughter: Women Speak Out* has enabled you to understand more clearly your own mother-daughter relationships. Here's what I personally learned from my own research and reflection:

- Being a woman in today's world is more challenging and exciting than it has ever been in the past. We have the opportunity to write new chapters about what it means to be a Christian woman.
- Our mother-daughter relationships are worthy of all the time and effort that we can devote to them. We will deeply regret doing anything less.

- We want more from our mothers than they are ever able to give us, and becoming aware of this pitfall should help us manage the relationships we have with our own daughters.
- Mending broken relationships should be a high priority in our lives. Estrangement and broken relationships affect our health, our feelings of self-worth, our Christian witness, and our ability to grow as women and move forward through life. God expects forgiveness and will help us to make it a reality in our lives.

For more information . . .

Caplan, Paula. *Don't Blame Mother: Mending the Mother-Daughter Relationship*. New York: Harper & Row, 1989.

Firman, Julie and Dorothy Firman. *Daughters and Mothers: Healing the Relationship*. New York: Continuum Publishing, 1990.

Strom, Kay Marshall. *Making Friends with Your Mother: A Book for Daughters*. Grand Rapids: Zondervan Publishing House, 1991.

Epilogue

❦

I'VE RECENTLY RETURNED FROM A VISIT TO A SOUTHERN CITY. I
spent two days with my younger sister, her husband, and three
children. While visits between sisters are not uncommon, this one
held the possibility for me of reconciliation, forgiveness, and understanding—or of recrimination, blame, and rejection.

We were virtual strangers, my sister and I. Estrangement, my
choice for over two decades, had separated us. I had fuzzy snapshots
of her in my mind based on brief encounters through the years—her
grief and despair at our father's funeral; her anger and hostility at our
mother's funeral. We had never spoken as sisters. I wrote to ask for a
meeting. She responded in the affirmative. I found myself alternating
between euphoria and apprehension as the plane approached the
runway. Would I even like this woman?

I was greeted warmly by my sister and her husband, a pastoral
psychologist. They hugged me and the tension left my body. We
spoke of the mundane as we drove to their home—the weather, our

❦

children, plans for the coming day. But it was an easy conversation. I felt welcomed and affirmed.

Throughout the weekend we talked. Through a nearly five-hour lunch we shared our perspectives on growing up. The ten-year difference in our ages made for vastly different impressions of how we were raised. I remembered a close and loving father. She remembered an absent one. I remembered a lonely childhood with few companions. She remembered our three next-door cousins, her constant playmates. We shared a common joy in the wide-open spaces and freedom of exploration that we enjoyed as children. She remembered only the closed doors and whispered conversations when I married someone against my parents' wishes. I explained what had happened from my perspective. I felt her anguish at being left on her own when my mother remarried, and I lamented my lack of support and encouragement for her.

Exploring her warmly decorated home with pieces of furniture from our childhood home and family pictures and memorabilia everywhere, I was reminded of an incident that stood out in my memory. A beautiful mahogany table stood before a window with an attractive arrangement of African violets on top of it.

"Do you know the story about me and this table?" I asked Kathy. She shook her head. "When I was eleven years old and you were just a baby," I told her, "I severely damaged this table." She looked at me in surprise. "Here," I said, "let's take off the plants and lift up the drop leaf." As we did so, I told her of the time I'd come running down the hall and crashed into the table. "The impact caused the top to fall down on two glass hurricane lamps and completely mar the inside surface. After that Mom never lifted the top again."

My sister was astounded to see the deep gouges and scratches inside. Someone had covered them with stain, but running my hands across the surface revealed that time had not healed these wounds. In a near antique they did not seem out of character. But when I was ten, the damage seemed irreparable, and both my mother and I were inconsolable.

My sister and I didn't speak of the symbolism. She enjoyed hearing the amusing story, and I enjoyed sharing it. I was pleased that the table played such a prominent part in her decor. But I have reflected on that table often since my return. Sometimes the wounds and gouges of our past experiences remain hidden away and we fail to expose them to the bright sunshine of Christ's love and forgiveness. We do not recognize that they can bring a beauty and dimension to our lives if we use them to grow and change. That table for me has become a metaphor for God's acceptance of me just as I am and a metaphor for my own acceptance of my mother, my sister, and myself.

I thought perhaps this brief exchange would be the high point of my visit. It seemed such a special moment. But there was to be one more. Before I was about to climb the stairs for bed that evening I peeked into the living room. Jenny, my twelve-year-old niece, was sitting at the piano. She was fingering the keys idly, and I sat down beside her. We exchanged stories of piano lessons and recitals, and she asked if I would play. The hymnal was inviting, and I selected a favorite I'd played often as a pianist for church services. I added some embellishments to the written music and Jenny was admiring. I began to play more, and soon my sister joined us. Her clear soprano began to sing the favorite hymns from both of our childhoods. I'd never had the opportunity to accompany her. Soon little Anne, the three-year-old, climbed down the stairs. The music was a magnet. We added some favorite choruses to the sing-a-long, and soon our four voices were united. I wanted those moments to go on forever. The spirit of God was touching my heart, and I mourned for the lost years and special moments I had missed because of my pride.

❦

There was one more extraordinarily important thing I discovered during my visit. I'm a keen observer of parenting styles. And I thoroughly enjoyed watching my sister parent her three children, ages 12, 6, and 3. As I listened to their conversational exchanges and observed her warmth, caring, and respect for them, I felt as though I was listening to myself. She was doing what I had always done. She was saying the same things I said as a parent. Suddenly I realized that I was watching my mother.

My mother had given us those wonderful gifts of affirmation, acceptance, caring, and respect. She had done that for us, and we were able to do it for our children. In my haste to blame and separate from my mother I had failed to affirm and recognize that my ability to write books about parenting, my ability to teach children with patience, and my ability to respect each child as an individual came from her. She was the one who had passed this wonderful gift to us. I only realized it as I watched Kathy interact with her children. I only regretted that it was too late to tell my mother in person.

❧

Appendix A

MOTHER-DAUGHTER QUESTIONNAIRE

1. DEMOGRAPHICS
How old are you?

How many daughters do you have?

How old is (are) your daughter(s)?

Do you have sons?

How many?

How old are they?

How old is your mother?

If deceased, how old were you when your mother died?

Did your father remarry?

How old were you?

Comments:

2. MARITAL STATUS OF RESPONDENT
Answer the section of Question 2 that pertains to your marital status.

2A. RESPONDENT MARRIED TO FIRST HUSBAND
How long have you been married?

Comments:

2B. RESPONDENT WIDOWED
How long have you been widowed?

How old was your daughter(s) when your husband died?

Comments:

2C. RESPONDENT DIVORCED
How old was your daughter when you divorced?

Comments:

2D. RESPONDENT DIVORCED AND REMARRIED
How old was your daughter when you divorced?

How old was your daughter when you remarried?

Comments:

2E. RESPONDENT SINGLE NEVER MARRIED

Are you the natural or adoptive mother of your daughter(s)?

If adopted, does your daughter(s) have contact with her natural mother?

If natural, does your daughter have contact with her father?

Comments:

3. EDUCATION

What is your highest degree?

What is your mother's highest degree?

What is your daughter's present educational status?

Did your mother attend a Christian college?

Did you attend a Christian college?

Does your daughter(s) attend a Christian college?

Comments:

❦

4. WOMEN'S LIBERATION/FEMINISM

How would you characterize your views toward "women's liberation"?

How would you characterize your mother's views?

Your daughter's views?

Comments:

5. ROLE OF WOMEN IN THE CHURCH

What role does (did) your mother play in the church?

What role have you played in the church?

What role does your daughter play in the church (if old enough)?

Comments:

6. EMPLOYMENT HISTORY

What jobs have you held?

During which stages of your daughter's life have your worked? (preschool age? school age? post-graduation age?)

What jobs has your mother held?

Did she work during your preschool age? school age? post-graduation age?

What jobs has your daughter(s) held?

❧

If your daughter has children has she worked during preschool age? school age? post-graduation age?

Comments:

7. *MARRIAGE*
What views of marriage did you get from your mother/father?

Are these the same views you have passed on to your daughter?

IF APPLICABLE: How is your daughter's marriage different from yours?

Comments:

8. *MONEY*
What part does (did) money play in your relationship with your mother?

What part does (did) money play in your relationship with your daughter?

9. *FOOD*
What part did food play in the relationship between you and your mother?

What part has food played in the relationship between you and your daughter?

Comments:

10. SPIRITUAL VALUES
How did your mother share spiritual values with you?

How do you share them with your daughter?

Are spiritual values/church attendance/choice of church a source of conflict between you and either your mother or daughter?

How do you handle this conflict?

11. ROLE OF FATHER/HUSBAND WITH DAUGHTERS
What part did your father play in the relationship with you and your mother?

What part does your husband play in the relationship between you and your daughter?

What part does (did) your daughter's husband play in your relationship with her?

Comments:

12. RELATIONSHIP WITH MOTHER
Characterize your relationship with your mother during the following periods of your life by checking one of the choices (Excellent, Good, Rocky, Non-Existent)

	Excellent	Good	Rocky	Non-Existent
Early Years				

Adolescence

Young Adulthood

Present

Comments:

13. RELATIONSHIP WITH DAUGHTER(S)

Characterize your relationship with your daughter(s) during the following periods of her life by checking one of the choices. If you have more than one daughter and the relationships are different, mark in different colors.

	Excellent	*Good*	*Rocky*	*Non-Existent*
Early Years				
Adolescence				
Young Adulthood				
Present				

Comments:

14. MOTHERS AS ROLE MODELS

In what way(s) are you most different from your mother?

❧

In what way(s) are you most different from your daughter?

Does your husband ever note similarities between you and your mother (in either a positive or negative way)?

Does your husband (or your daughter's husband) ever note similarities between you and your daughter (in either a positive or negative way)?

Comments:

15. POSITIVES/NEGATIVES
What do you like best about your mother?

What do you like least about your mother?

What do you like best about your daughter?

What do you like least about your daughter?

Comments:

16. CONFLICT
What is the biggest point of conflict between you and your mother? (Now or in the past)

What is the biggest point of conflict between you and your daughter? (Now or in the past)

Comments:

17. Choose the question from 17A-17F that applies to you. If you have daughters in several categories, complete all categories that apply to you. If you have several daughters in one category, generalize or use different-colored pencils to answer.

17A. MOTHERS OF YOUNG DAUGHTERS (0-12)
What do you wish most for your daughter as she matures?

What worries you most about the future for your daughter?

Comments:

17B. MOTHERS OF ADOLESCENT DAUGHTERS (13-18)
What do you wish most for your daughter in the future?

What has been the worst part of parenting an adolescent daughter?

What has been the best part of parenting an adolescent daughter?

Comments:

17C. MOTHERS OF SINGLE DAUGHTERS (never married or divorced) (ages 20+)
What do you wish most for your daughter in the future?

Does it bother you that she is not married?

Do you ever discuss these issues?

Have you ever worried that she might be gay? Have you ever discussed the issue?

Comments:

17D. MOTHERS OF MARRIED DAUGHTERS WITHOUT CHILDREN
What do you wish most for your daughter in the future?

Has your relationship with your daughter changed since she married?

Do you and your husband approve of her husband?

Do you ever discuss her having children?

Comments:

17E. MOTHERS OF MARRIED DAUGHTERS WITH CHILDREN (grandchildren)
How did your daughter's having children change your relationship with her?

What do you wish most for your daughter in the future?

Comments:

18. FUTURE
What one thing would you wish to be different for your daughter than what you have experienced in your life?

❦

Comments:

19. SEX
How did your mother handle discussing sex with you?

How did you handle it with your daughter?

How would you characterize your relationship with your mother when it comes to sharing intimate details?

Does your daughter discuss intimate details of her life with you?

If this relationship is different than what you had with your mother, why do you think this has happened?

Comments:

20. OTHER RELATIONSHIPS
Does your daughter have any "other mothers" (older women who act as mentors and confidantes)?

Do you have any "other daughters" (younger women with whom you spend time and who confide in you)?

Do you have any "other mothers"?

Do you have any daughter-in-laws? How is your relationship with them different from your own daughters?

Describe your relationships with your own mother-in-law.

Comments:

21. ESTRANGEMENT

Have you ever been estranged from your mother for any length of time?

What do you think are the reasons for this estrangement?

How have you handled it?

What have you done to attempt reconciliation?

Have you consulted any sources for help? Books? Counselor?

Have you ever been estranged from your daughter for any length of time?

What do you think are the reasons for this estrangement?

How have you handled it?

What have you done to attempt reconciliation?

Have you consulted any sources for help? Books? Counselor?

Comments:

22. HABITS AND BEHAVIOR

What one thing would you like your mother to stop doing?

❦

What one thing would you like your mother to start doing?

What one thing would you like your daughter to stop doing?

What one thing would you like your daughter to start doing?

Comments:

23. SHARED INTERESTS/ACTIVITIES
What do you typically do together as mother/daughter (your mother)?

What do you typically do together as mother/daughter (your daughter)?

24. CARETAKER ROLE
Have you ever been or are you now in a caretaking role with your mother?

Describe.

How has this changed your relationship?

Comments:

25. REGRETS
What would you do differently in your relationship with your mother if given the opportunity?

What would you do differently in your relationship with your daughter if given the opportunity?

❧

26. PASSAGES/STAGES/CHANGES IN LIFE
From your perspective has your mother changed or gone through stages or passages of growth in her life, or is she the same today as you remember her growing up?

Have you gone through any significant changes/stages/passages in your life?

Comments:

27. TYPOLOGY
Theorists have hypothesized five types of mother-daughter relationships:

I. *Responsible Mother/Dependent Daughter*: mothers cater to daughters' emotional and physical needs

II. *Responsible Daughter/Dependent Mother:* daughters are far more likely to give than receive help from mothers

III. *Peerlike Friendship:* high involvement in each other's lives and a strong norm for independence

IV. *Mutual Mothering:* sense of mutual responsibility or protectiveness; much involvement in each other's activities; telephone/visit daily; visit in each other's homes often

V. *Uninvolved:* lack of emotional involvement; does not fit into any of the other types

❦

Which of the five typologies characterizes your relationship with your mother?

Which type characterizes your relationship with your daughter (if old enough to make comment)?

Comments:

28. MISCELLANEOUS
Do you have a special tribute for your mother you would like to have included in this book?

Do you have a special tribute to your daughter you would like to have included in this book?

Appendix B

SUMMARY OF QUESTIONNAIRE RESULTS

AGE CATEGORIES OF RESPONDENTS

	n	*%*
25-35	12	14
36-45	34	39
46-55	24	27
56-65	12	14
66-75	6	6
Total	88	100

AGE CATEGORIES OF RESPONDENTS' MOTHERS

Mothers ranged in age from 49 to 99.

Twenty-one of the respondents' mothers were deceased. Two lost

mothers in infancy, two in childhood, eight in young adulthood, and
two in middle-age. Four respondents were reared by stepmothers and
one by a maternal grandmother.

MARITAL STATUS OF RESPONDENTS

	n	%
Happily Married	24	33
Neutral Married	44	61
Unhappily Married	4	6
Total	72	100

Of the seventy-two respondents who were married, four made specific statements relative to the negative quality of their marriages
that impacted the relationships they had with their daughters.
Twenty-four made specific statements about the positive qualities of
their marriages that impacted relationships they had with their
daughters. Forty-four of the respondents made no specific references
to the impact of their marriages on the relationships with daughters.

	n	%
Married	72	82
Widowed	1	1
Widowed/Remarried	2	2
Single Never Married	1	1
Divorced/Remarried	8	9
Divorced	4	5
Total	88	100

❦

EDUCATIONAL STATUS

	n	%
High School Diploma	10	11
High School + Some College	9	10
Bachelor's Degree	37	42
R.N.	6	7
Master's Degree	22	26
Doctorate Degree	4	4
Total	88	100

RELIGIOUS AFFILIATION

	n	%
Evangelical Christian	45	51
Protestant	21	25
Catholic	9	10
Jewish	3	3
No professed church or religious beliefs	10	11
Total	88	100

EMPLOYMENT STATUS

	n	%
Never Worked After HS/College	4	5
Worked Before Marriage or Children Not Worked When Children		

Were Young (Preschool) Resumed Working/Now Working	39	44
Worked Before Marriage or Children/Working Part-Time or in Home	11	13
Worked Before Marriage or Children/Not Working Now	18	20
Worked Before Children Continued to Work through Rearing Children	16	18
Total	88	100

BREAKDOWN OF DAUGHTERS OF EIGHTY-EIGHT SUBJECTS

The eighty-eight subjects had a total of 169 daughters.

	n	*%*
One Daughter	41	47
Two Daughters	24	27
Three Daughters	14	16
Four Daughters	7	8
Five Daughters	2	2
Total	88	100

BREAKDOWN OF AGES OF 169 DAUGHTERS

Young Daughters	42
Adolescent Daughters	42
Single Daughters	36

❧

Divorced/Remarried (no children)	3
Divorced/Not Remarried (no children)	4
Divorced/Remarried (children)	1
Divorced/Not Remarried (children)	2
Married (no children)	10
Married (children)	29
Total	169

STATUS OF RELATIONSHIP WITH MOTHER

	n	%
Outstanding	30	38
Average	39	49
Poor	10	13
Total	79	100

Some respondents whose mothers were deceased did not complete the status of relationship portion of the questionnaire, while others whose mothers had died more recently did so. This accounts for the difference in number of total respondents and number indicated above.

STATUS OF RELATIONSHIP WITH YOUNG DAUGHTERS (0-12)

	n	%
Outstanding	40	95
Average	2	5
Total	42	100

❧

STATUS OF RELATIONSHIP WITH ADOLESCENT DAUGHTERS (13-18)

	n	%
Outstanding	10	24
Average	30	71
Poor	2	5
Total	42	100

STATUS OF RELATIONSHIP WITH YOUNG ADULT DAUGHTERS (early 20s)

	n	%
Outstanding	18	38
Average	25	52
Poor	5	10
Total	48	100

STATUS OF RELATIONSHIP WITH ADULT DAUGHTERS (over 25)

	n	%
Outstanding	18	49
Average	16	43
Poor	3	8
Total	37	100

❦

Notes

Chapter One

1. Ann Oakley, *Women Confined: Toward a Sociology of Childbirth* (Oxford: Martin Robertson, 1980).

2. J. Brooks-Gunn and Wendy Schempp Matthews, *He and She: How Children Develop Their Sex-Role Identity* (Englewood Cliffs, N.J.: Prentice-Hall, 1979), 72.

3. J. Brooks-Gunn, "The Relationship of Maternal Beliefs about Sex-Typing to Maternal and Young Children's Behavior." Paper prepared for the International Conference on Infancy Study, 1984.

4. Ramona Mercer, et al, *Transitions in a Woman's Life: Major Life Events in Developmental Context* (New York: Springer Publishing Company, 1989).

5. Ibid, 75-83.

6. Susan Price, *The Female Ego: The Hidden Power Women Possess but Are Afraid to Use* (New York: Rawson Associates, 1984).

Chapter Two

1. Karen Johnson, *Trusting Ourselves: The Sourcebook on Psychology for Women* (New York: The Atlantic Monthly Press, 1990).

Chapter Three

1. Elizabeth Fishel, *Family Mirrors: What Our Children's Lives Reveal about Ourselves* (Boston: Houghton Mifflin, 1991), 95.

2. Judith M. Bardwick, ed., *Readings on the Psychology of Women* (New York: Harper & Row, 1972), 22-29.

3. Lois Wladis Hoffman, "Early Childhood Experiences and Women's Achievement Motives," *Journal of Social Issues* (2 February, 1972), 129-55.

4. S.R. Vogel, I. Broverman, D. Broverman, F. Clarkson, and P. Rosenkrantz, "Maternal Employment and Perceptions of Sex-Role Stereotypes," *Developmental Psychology* 3 (1970): 384-91.

Chapter Four

1. Daniel Offer, *The Psychological World of the Teenager: A Study of Normal Adolescent Boys* (New York: Basic Books, 1969).

2. Gisela Konopka, *Young Girls: A Portrait of Adolescence* (Englewood Cliffs, N.J.: Prentice Hall, 1976).

3. Richard M. Lerner, "A Life-Span Perspective for Early Adolescence," in R. Lerner and T.L. Foch, eds., *Biological-Psychosocial Interactions in Early Adolescence* (Hillsdale, N.J.: Lawrence Erlbaum, 1987).

4. Terri Apter, *Altered Loves: Mothers and Daughters During Adolescence* (New York: St. Martin's Press, 1990), 60.

5. Ibid., 71.

6. Kristen A. Moore, James L. Peterson, and Frank F. Furstenberg, "Parental Attitudes and the Occurrence of Early Sexual Activity," *Journal of Marriage and the Family* 48 (1986).

7. Ann Caron, *Don't Stop Loving Me: A Reassuring Guide for Mothers of Adolescent Daughters* (New York: Holt, 1990), 179.

8. Catherine R. Cooper, "Role of Conflict in Adolescent-Parent Relationships," in Gunnar and Collins, eds., *Development During the Transition to Adolescence* (Hillside, N.J.: Lawrence Erlbaum, 1988).

9. Earl S. Schaefer, "A Circumplex Model for Maternal Behavior," *Journal of Abnormal and Social Psychology* 59 (1959).

❦

Chapter Five

1. Sumru Erkut, "Daughters Talking About Their Mothers: A View from the Campus," Working Paper No. 127 (Wellesley, Mass.: Wellesley College Center for Research on Women), 16.

2. Ibid., p. 16.

3. Nancy Doyle Chalfant, *Child of Grace* (Wheaton, Ill.: Harold Shaw Publishers, 1988).

4. Susan McGee Bailey, "Old Messages, New Circumstances," Working Paper No. 210 (Wellesley, Mass.: Wellesley College Center for Research on Women, 1990).

5. Erkut, 16.

Chapter Six

1. Rosalind C. Barnett, "Adult Daughters and Their Mothers: Harmony or Hostility," Working Paper No. 209 (Wellesley, Mass.: Wellesley College Center for Research on Women, 1990).

2. B.J. Cohler and H.U. Grunebaum, *Mothers, Grandmothers, and Daughters: Personality and Child Care in Three-Generation Families* (New York: John Wiley & Sons, Inc., 1981).

3. Barnett, op. cit.

4. Lucy R. Fischer, *Linked Lives: Adult Daughters and their Mothers* (New York: Harper & Row, 1986), 47.

5. Ibid., 56.

6. Barnett, op. cit., 9.

7. Ibid.

8. Cohler, op. cit., 89.

Chapter Seven

1. Victoria Secunda, *When You and Your Mother Can't Be Friends: Resolving the Most Complicated Relationship of Your Life* (New York: Delacorte Press, 1990), xxi.

2. Secunda, op. cit., 81-159.

3. Ibid., 82.

4. Ibid., 119.

5. Ibid., 129.

6. Ibid., 131.

7. Ibid., 146.

8. Ibid.

9. Ibid., 184.

10. Ibid., 205.

11. Ibid., 260.

12. Paula Caplan, *Don't Blame Mother: Mending the Mother-Daughter Relationship* (New York: Harper & Row, 1989), 193.

13. Mary Pride, *The Way Home: Beyond Feminism, Back to Reality* (Wheaton, Ill.: Crossway Books, 1985).

14. Caplan, op. cit., 84.

15. Jain Sherrard. *Mother-Warrior-Pilgrim* (Kansas City, Mo.: Andres and McMel, 1980).

16. Secunda, op. cit., 96-127.

17. Kim Chernin. *Reinventing Eve* (New York: Random House, 1987).

18. Janet Surrey, "The 'Self-in-Relation': A Theory of Women's Development." Paper No. 13 (Wellesley, Mass.: Wellesley College Center for Research on Women, 1985).

Chapter Eight

1. Paula Caplan, *Don't Blame Mother: Mending the Mother-Daughter Relationship* (New York: Harper & Row, 1989), 147.

2. Ibid., 163.

3. Victoria Secunda, *When You and Your Mother Can't Be Friends: Resolving the Most Complicated Relationship of Your Life* (New York: Delacorte Press, 1990), 311.

4. Kay Marshall Strom *Making Friends With Your Mother* (Grand Rapids, Mich.: Zondervan Publishing, 1991).

5. Secunda, op. cit., 363.

6. Julie Firman and Dorothy Firman, *Daughters and Mothers: Healing the Relationship* (New York: Continuum, 1989), 172.

7. Ibid., 211-220.

Bibliography

Abramson, Jane B. *Mothermania: A Psychological Study of Mother-Daughter Conflict.* Lexington Books, 1986.

Adeney, Miriam. *A Time for Risking.* Portland, Oreg.: Multnomah Press, 1987.

Alexander, Jo, Debi Berrow, Lisa Domitrovich, Margarita Donnelly, and Cheryl McLean, eds. *Women and Aging.* Corvallis, Oreg.: Calyx Books, 1986.

Apter, Terri. *Altered Loves: Mothers and Daughters During Adolescence.* New York: St. Martin's Press, 1990.

Arcana, Judith. *Our Mothers' Daughters.* Berkeley, Calif.: Shameless Hussy Press, 1979.

Arnstein, Helene S. *Between Mothers-In-Law & Daughters-In-Law: Achieving a Successful and Caring Relationship.* Dodd, 1987.

————. *Getting Along with Your Grown-Up Children.* Philadelphia: M. Evans and Company, Inc., 1970.

Bailey, Susan McGee. "Old Messages, New Circumstances." Working Paper No. 210. Wellesley, Mass.: Wellesley College Center for Research on Women, 1990.

Bandinter, Elizabeth. *Mother Love: Myth and Reality*. New York: Macmillan, 1980.

Barnett, Rosalind C. "Adult Daughters and Their Mothers: Harmony or Hostility?" Working Paper No. 209. Wellesley, Mass.: Wellesley College Center for Research on Women, 1990.

Barnett, Rosalind C., Nazli Kibria, Grace K. Baruch, and Joseph H. Pleck. "Quality of Adult Daughters' Relationships with their Mothers and Fathers: Effects on Daughters' Well-Being and Psychological Distress." Working Paper No. 175. Wellesley, Mass.: Wellesley College Center for Research on Women, 1988.

Bassoff, Evelyn. *Mothers and Daughters: Loving and Letting Go*. New York: New American Library, 1988.

————. *Mothering Ourselves: Help and Healing for Adult Daughters*. Dutton, 1990.

Bence, Evelyn. *Leaving Home*. Wheaton, Ill.: Tyndale House Publishers, Inc., 1986.

Bird, Caroline. *Born Female: The High Cost of Keeping Woman Down*. New York: David McKay Company, Inc., 1970.

Birns, B. and D. Hay, eds. *The Different Faces of Motherhood*. New York: Plenum Press, 1988.

Block, Joel D. and Diane Greenberg. *Women and Friendship*. New York: Franklin Watts, 1985.

Bloomfield, Harold H. *Making Peace with Your Parents*. New York: Random House, 1983.

Boulton, M.G. *On Being a Mother: A Study of Women with Preschool Children*. London: Tavistock Publications, 1983.

❦

Brans, Jo. *Mother, I Have Something to Tell You: Understanding Your Child's Chosen Lifestyle.* Garden City, N.Y.: Doubleday & Company, 1987.

Brazelton, T. Berry. *Infants and Mothers: Differences in Development.* New York: Delacorte Press, 1969.

Brody, Elaine. *Women in the Middle: Their Parent-Care Years.* New York: Springer Publishing Company, 1990.

Burck, Frances Wells. *Mothers Talking: Sharing the Secret.* New York: St. Martin's Press, 1986.

Caplan, Paula J. *Between Women: Lowering the Barriers.* Toronto: Spectrum Publications, 1981.

———. *Barriers Between Women.* New York: SP Medical & Scientific Books, 1981.

———. *Don't Blame Mother: Mending the Mother-Daughter Relationship.* New York: Harper & Row, 1989.

Caron, Ann F. *"Don't Stop Loving Me" : A Reassuring Guide for Mothers of Adolescent Daughters.* New York: Holt, 1990.

Chase, Janet. *Daughters of Change: Growing Up Female in America.* Boston: Little, Brown and Company, 1981.

Chesler, Phyllis. *With Child: A Diary of Motherhood.* New York: Thomas Y. Crowell, Publishers, 1979.

Chess, Stella and Jane Whitbread. *Daughters: From Infancy to Independence.* Garden City, N.Y.: Doubleday & Company, Inc., 1978.

Chodorow, Nancy. *The Reproduction of Mothering: Psychoanalysis and the Sociology of Gender.* Berkley: University of California Press, 1978.

Coleman, Sheila Schuller. *Between Mother and Daughter.* Old Tappan, N.J.: Fleming H. Revell Company, 1982.

Cooper, Jane, ed. *Extended Outlooks: The Iowa Review Collection of Contemporary Women Writers.* New York: Macmillan, n.d.

Curtis, Patricia. *Why Isn't My Daughter Married?* Los Angeles: Price Stern Sloan, 1988.

Davidson, Cathy N. and E.M. Broner, eds. *The Lost Tradition: Mothers and Daughters in Literature.* New York: Frederick Ungar Publishing Co., 1980.

Dowling, Colette. *Perfect Women: Hidden Fears of Inadequacy and the Drive to Perform.* New York: Summit Books, 1988.

Dunn, Rita and Kenneth Dunn. *How to Raise Independent and Professionally Successful Daughters.* Englewood Cliffs, N.J.: Prentice Hall, Inc., 1977.

Edwards, Lee R., Mary Heath, and Lisa Baskin, eds. *Woman: An Issue.* Boston: Little, Brown and Company, 1972.

Eichenbaum, Louise and Susie Orbach. *Between Women.* New York: Viking, 1988.

⸻. *Outside In . . . Inside Out.* Harmondsworth: Penguin, 1982.

⸻. *Understanding Women.* Harmondsworth: Penguin, 1985.

⸻. *What Do Women Want?* London: Fontana, 1984.

Erkut, Sumru. "Daughters Talking About Their Mothers: A View from the Campus." Working Paper No. 127. Wellesley, Mass.: Wellesley College Center for Research on Women, 1984.

Firman, Julie and Dorothy Firman. *Daughters and Mothers: Healing the Relationship.* New York: Continuum, 1989.

Fischer, Lucy R. *Linked Lives: Adult Daughters and Their Mothers.* San Francisco: Harper & Row, 1986.

Fishel, Elizabeth. *Family Mirrors: What Our Children's Lives Reveal about Ourselves.* Boston: Houghton Mifflin, 1991.

Fisher, Florence. *The Search for Anna Fisher.* New York: Arthur Fields Books, Inc., 1973.

Frailberg, Selma. *Every Child's Birthright: In Defense of Mothering.* New York: Basic Books, 1977.

❧

Friday, Nancy. *My Mother, Myself: A Daughter's Search for Identity.* New York: Delacorte Press, 1977.

Gee, Ellen M. and Meredith M. Kimball. *Women and Aging.* Toronto: Butterworths, 1987.

Gordon, Jacquie. *Give Me One Wish.* New York: W.W. Norton & Company, 1988.

Gornick, Vivian. *Fierce Attachments.* New York: Farrar, Straus & Giroux, Inc., 1987.

Gross, Zenith Henkin. *And You Thought It Was All Over!* New York: St. Martin's Press, 1985.

Gundry, Patricia. *Woman Be Free!* Grand Rapids, Mich.: Zondervan Publishing House, 1977.

Hammer, Signe. *Daughters and Mothers: Mothers and Daughters.* New York: Quadrangel/The New York Times Book Co., 1975.

Hartman, Susan M. *The Home Front and Beyond: American Women in the 1940s.* Boston: Twayne Publishers, 1982.

Heilbrun, Carolyn G. *Reinventing Womanhood.* New York: W.W. Norton & Company, 1979.

Josselson, Ruthelien. *Finding Herself: Pathways to Identity Development In Women.* San Francisco: Jossey-Bass Publishers, 1983.

Kitzinger, Sheila. *Women as Mothers: How They See Themselves in Different Cultures.* New York: Random House, 1978.

Kippelman, Susan, ed. *Between Mothers & Daughters: Stories Across a Generation.* Old Westbury, N.Y.: Feminist Press, 1984.

Lazarre, Jan. *The Mother Knot.* New York: McGraw-Hill Book Company, 1976.

Leifer, Myra. *The Psychological Effects of Motherhood: A Study of First Pregnancy.* New York: Praeger, 1980.

Lerner, Gerda, ed. *The Female Experience: An American Documentary.* Indianapolis: Bobbs-Merrill Educational Publishing, 1977.

Lifshin, Lyn, ed. *Tangled Vines: A Collection of Mother and Daughter Poems.* Boston: Beacon Press, 1978.

Logan, Margaret. *Happy Endings.* Boston: Houghton Mifflin Company, 1979.

Margolis, Maxine E. *Mothers & Such: Views of American Women & Why They Changed.* Berkley: University of California Press, 1984.

Martin, Faith. *Call Me Blessed: The Emerging Christian Woman.* Grand Rapids, Mich.: William B. Eerdmans Publishing Co., 1988.

Mercer, Ramona T. *First-Time Motherhood: Experiences from Teens to Forties.* New York: Springer Publishing, 1986.

Mercer, Ramona T., Elizabeth G. Nichols, Glen Caspers Doyle. *Transitions in a Woman's Life: Major Life Events in Developmental Context.* New York: Springer Publishing, 1989.

Mitchell, Juliet and Ann Oakley, eds. *What Is Feminism: A Reexamination.* New York: Pantheon Books, 1986.

Neisser, Edith G. *Mothers and Daughters: A Lifelong Relationship.* New York: Harper & Row, 1967.

Newsweek. "The Daughter Track." July 16, 1990.

Olsen Tillie. *Mother to Daughter: Daughter to Mother.* Old Westbury, N.Y.: Feminist Press, 1984.

Payne Karen, ed. *Between Ourselves: Letters between Mothers and Daughters.* Boston: Houghton Miffl n Company, 1983.

Powell, Barbara. *How to Raise a Successful Daughter.* Chicago: Nelson Hall, 1979.

Price, June. *Motherhood: What It Does to Your Mind.* New York: Pandora Press, 1989.

Pride, Mary. *The Way Home: Beyond Feminism, Back to Reality.* Wheaton, Ill.: Crossway Books, 1985.

Rafkin, Louise, ed. *Different Daughters: A Book by Mothers of Lesbians.* Pittsburgh: Cleis Press, 1987.

Rich, Adrienne. *Of Woman Born: Motherhood as Experience and Institution*. New York: W.W. Norton & Company, 1976.

Rivers, Caryl, Rosalind Barnett, and Grace Baruch. *Beyond Sugar and Spice: How Women Grow, Learn and Thrive*. New York: G.P. Putnam's Sons, 1979.

Rothman, S.M. *Woman's Proper Place: A History of Changing Ideals and Practice, 1870 to the Present*. New York: Basic Books, 1978.

Ryan, Mary P. *Womanhood in America: From Colonial Times to the Present*. New York: Franklin Watts, 1983.

Sanford, Linda Tshirhart and Mary Ellen Donovan. *Women and Self-Esteem: Understanding and Improving the Way We Think and Feel about Ourselves*. Garden City, N.Y.: Anchor Press/Doubleday, 1984.

Schultz, Susan P. *To My Daughter with Love*. New York: Warner Books, 1988.

Secunda, Victoria. *When You and Your Mother Can't Be Friends: Resolving the Most Complicated Relationship of Your Life*. New York: Delacorte Press, 1990.

Shreve, Anita. *Remaking Motherhood: How Working Mothers Are Shaping Our Children's Future*. New York: Viking, 1987.

Sidel, Ruth. *On Her Own: Growing Up in the Shadow of the American Dream*. New York: Viking, 1990.

Sluckin, Wladyslaw, Martin Herbert, and Alice Sluckin. *Maternal Bonding*. Oxford: Basil Blackwell, 1984.

Smith, Liz. *The Mother Book*. Garden City, N.Y.: Doubleday & Company, Inc., 1978.

Spellman, Cathy Cash. *Notes to My Daughters*. New York: Crown Publishers, Inc., 1981.

Spignesi, Angelyn. *Starving Women: A Psychology of Anorexia*. Dallas: Spring, 1983.

Strecker, Edward A., M.D. and Vincent T. Lathbury, M.D. *Their Mothers' Daughters*. Philadelphia: J.B. Lippincott Company, 1956.

Strom, Kay Marshall. *Making Friends with Your Mother: A Book for Daughters*. Grand Rapids, Mich.: Zondervan Publishing House, 1991.

Strom, Kay and Lisa Strom. *Mothers and Daughters Together: We Can Work It Out*. Grand Rapids, Mich.: Baker Book House, 1988.

Wandersee, Winifred D. *American Women in the 1970's: On the Move*. Boston: Twayne Publishers, 1988.

Ware, Susan. *American Women in the 1930s: Holding Their Own*. Boston: Twayne Publishers, 1982.